Ready, Set, Organize!

SECOND EDITION

A Workbook for the Organizationally Challenged

Pipi Campbell Peterson, with Mary Campbell

Park Avenue

Ready, Set, Organize! Second Edition
A Workbook for the Organizationally Challenged

© 2002 by Pipi Campbell Peterson

Published by Park Avenue, an imprint of JIST Publishing, Inc.
8902 Otis Avenue
Indianapolis, IN 46216-1033
Phone: 1-800-648-JIST   Fax: 1-800-JIST-FAX   E-Mail: editorial@jist.com

Visit our Web site at **www.jist.com** for information on JIST, free job search information, book chapters, and ordering information on our many products! Quantity discounts are available for JIST books. Please call our Sales Department at 1-800-648-5478 for a free catalog and more information.

Acquisitions and Development Editor: Lori Cates
Cover and Interior Designer: Aleata Howard
Interior Layout: Carolyn J. Newland
Proofreader: Paula Lowell
Indexer: Larry Sweazy

Printed in the United States of America.
06 05 04 03 02   9 8 7 6 5 4 3 2 1

Library of Congress Cataloging-in-Publication Data

Peterson, Pipi Campbell, 1940-
   Ready, set, organize! : a workbook for the organizationally challenged / Pipi Campbell
   Peterson with Mary Campbell.– 2nd ed.
       p. cm.
   Includes bibliographical references and index.
   ISBN 1-57112-111-0
   1. Time management. 2. Time management–Problems, exercises, etc. I. Campbell,
Mary. II. Title.

HD69.T54 P48 2001
650.1–dc21

                                                    2001036077

ISBN 1-57112-111-0

Dedication

To my parents, H. Dan and Melba Campbell, who always said I could and provided examples and opportunities for me to accomplish what I would.

Acknowledgments

What Would I Have Done Without...

Mary Campbell, my good friend and sister, and a talented writer and editor, without whom this book would still be a pile of paper.

Paul Curro, who had enough faith in me to read my writing and do something about it.

Barbara Hemphill, author and former president of the National Association of Professional Organizers (NAPO), as well as other professional organizers who have given this helping profession well-deserved status and recognition. Organizing does make a difference!

Brad Milton, my computer mentor, who to the best of his ability brought me up to speed on the electronic age.

The O'Kids: Jenny Campbell, Pete Fey, Robin Fey, Chloe Fortina, Desi Fortina, Skyler Lewis, Bridget McCartney, Browyn McCartney, Molly McCartney, Evan Milton, Lizzie Sharpe, Brent Sherman, Hanna Wanzenried, Marcy Wanzenried, Xela Warmer, Evan Westhoff, Katy Westhoff, Jason Witty, Tara Witty, and Kayci Zimmer.

Special Thanks To...

My husband Pete; my daughters, Christy and Paige; and son-in-law Kurt, for their humor, patience, creativity, and ideas.

My humorous and awesome brother John.

Wonderful grandchildren Katy, Evan, and Ellie for being inspiring and full of life.

Precious friends.

Contents

Part III: Organizing Your Household 129

Chapter 7: An Office in Every Home 131

Chapter 8: Organizing *of* the Children, *by* the Children, and *with* the Children 155

About This Book: Stuff to Know Before You Start

This book is about time and space and storage. You can learn to organize your time:

- ▲ not so you can do more, but so you can enjoy more of what you do;

- ▲ not so you can have complete control of your life (because that's impossible), but so you can manage what is manageable and know what isn't;

- ▲ and not so you can banish stress from your life (that's impossible too), but so you can reduce, counteract, and channel stress by planning (a weekly game of handball or an occasional bubble bath) and choosing (to resign from a committee that never was your cup of tea).

I invite you to be open to new ways of thinking about your time and your personal style. Do you strive for structure or treasure spontaneity? Which works best in your life?

I encourage you to organize your papers, clothing, and other possessions because knowing where things are and being able to get to them quickly might save you many hours and much frustration. If you need more help than I can give you in my book, don't despair. The National Association of Professional Organizers (of which I'm a member) has a referral and information hot line. For information on organizers in your area, call 512-206-0151 or visit the NAPO Web site at www.NAPO.net.

Be relieved that this book is not a set of rules. Instead, it is a workbook that guides you in determining the best use of your time and your space. You need no special skills or talents. This book presents organizing as a building process. Although this comprehensive approach to organizing takes time, you'll work—at your own pace—in steps that usually require just an hour or two, depending on the magnitude of your home, your family, and your possessions.

By following the step-by-step guidance in *Ready, Set, Organize!* you can complete each objective and chart your personal progress. Most chapters provide checklists so you can check off each task after you complete it.

Ready, Set, Organize! also includes worksheets for you to use and examples of how to complete them. But remember: There's no one right way to organize; incorporate the chapters' guidelines with your own methods—use whatever feels right to you. Be original, be creative, be flexible, take chances.

As an added bonus, a glossary of Pipi's "organizing terms" appears at the end of this book. You can refer to it if you run across a term that is unfamiliar to you.

This book provides ideas, techniques, and tools. You choose the ones that fit your situation best. You fill in the blanks. Finally, you carry out your plan.

Ready? Good! Let's organize.

Introduction

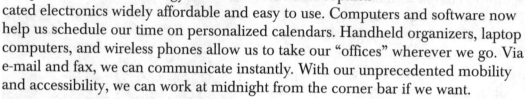

Since 1993, when I wrote *Ready, Set, Organize!*, changes in our world have made our lives at once easier and more complicated. The technology revolution has made sophisticated electronics widely affordable and easy to use. Computers and software now help us schedule our time on personalized calendars. Handheld organizers, laptop computers, and wireless phones allow us to take our "offices" wherever we go. Via e-mail and fax, we can communicate instantly. With our unprecedented mobility and accessibility, we can work at midnight from the corner bar if we want.

Is that good news? Well, yes and no. In these pages we'll examine the advantages and show you how to avoid the pitfalls.

A second change concerns the evolution of organizing as a profession. More than a thousand professional organizers are members of the National Association of Professional Organizers (NAPO) as of this writing. There are hundreds of new Web sites that deal with being organized, and new tools for organizing (time, money, and goods) enter the marketplace daily. Products and services to help you get organized are suggested throughout the book.

Moreover, we have seen heightened awareness of the value of organizing. Physicians and other health professionals are recognizing the importance of organizing techniques, not only for people with stress-related disorders, but also for children and adults with Attention Deficit Disorder and Chronic Disorganization. ADD and CD can undermine the ability of some people to function in their own homes. Embarrassed to have visitors and unable to manage their lives, they can become isolated and depressed.

Technology, combined with the growing sophistication of organizing and its uses, makes "getting your stuff together" more convenient, enjoyable, and necessary than ever. I hope this new edition of *Ready, Set, Organize!* will help you discover a new, more satisfying way to live.

Pipi Peterson
July 2001

Part I

Take Time to Find Time

Chapter 1

The Things That Matter Most

"Of all resources, time appears to be the least understood and the most mismanaged."

–R. Alec MacKenzie[1]

M any people believe that preparing a course of action–planning, in other words–limits their freedom. On the contrary, realistic planning allows you *more* freedom.

▲ **Planning makes life more enjoyable.** You can spend more time on your priorities and less time on things that aren't really important. Why spend two hours each September digging through papers for your children's inoculation records when you could be hot-air ballooning or saving the world? Most time-savers are easy to do. Putting up plastic hooks in the bathroom keeps towels off the floor and out of the laundry basket. Sorting mail as you look through it eliminates searching for your phone bill or the letter from Aunt Daggmar.

▲ **Planning prevents time-squandering emergencies.** You will spend less time "putting out fires" when you are able to anticipate and thus sidestep problems. By planning, you can avoid duplicating your efforts, bypass pitfalls, and discover where you waste your time. Knowing the steps to take and the proper sequence, you can get from A to Z without backtracking. It's better to prevent a crisis, or prepare for one, than to manage or be managed by one.

▲ **Planning aids decision-making by revealing the "big picture."** It's sort of like studying a jigsaw puzzle or a Rube Goldberg creation. Seeing how all the elements interact–possessions, people, money, and time–gives you a framework for your decisions. Day-to-day activities are more purposeful and effective. What to do and when to do it make more sense, and you stop procrastinating.

▲ **Planning is liberating.** "Time management" becomes "self-management" when you gain control of time, situations, tasks, and problems instead of allowing them to control you. You need to manage your time if you want to manage anything else.

This chapter lays the groundwork for a master plan for getting organized. Steps 1 through 5 will help you do the following:

▲ Develop long-term goals based on what is important to you.

▲ Set specific objectives for your goals.

▲ Plan activities that will accomplish your objectives.

Planning is more than a one-time effort; it's a way of life. Being organized requires planning and follow-up, but is much easier and more satisfying and effective than being unorganized. The benefits can be life-changing–even life-saving.

Organizing for Health and Serenity

Organize to lessen stress. Stress occurs when a situation or event–even a joyful one, such as having a baby–disrupts your routine enough to affect your mental and physical well-being. In the United States, stress drains $200 billion a year out of businesses' coffers–and ultimately consumers' pocketbooks–due to employee absenteeism, insurance claims, and lost productivity. Stress is implicated in half of all illnesses and up to 80 percent of doctor visits.[2]

You can't always foresee major life events and other changes that create stress. Besides, a certain amount of stress is essential for growth. But taking control of your daily routines can eliminate most harmful stress. "Disorganization probably wastes more time and creates more stress than any other single characteristic."[2] Organizing counteracts disorganization! Organizing consists of stress-prevention activities such as creating a communication center, dividing and conquering, and simplifying your life.

The role of health in disorganization can be powerful, as both a cause and an effect. In extreme cases, people virtually paralyzed by the inability to organize become clinically depressed. Others get angry or develop physical problems.

Disorganization has many causes and takes many forms. Some people are simply unaware of organizing techniques and tools. Some people believe they can rely on having "an organized mind." Others are organized at the office but not at home—possibly because the workplace offers tools, support, and structure that are not available at home.

Thus, no single organizing method works for everyone.

Many unconsciously resist becoming organized, whether it's because they will lose their excuse for underachieving, or they fear the lifestyle changes they may have to make. Or perhaps they have adapted so thoroughly to their chaotic way of doing things that it's tied to their self-image. They may like being called "ditzy" and wonder what will distinguish them when their lives are in order. Perhaps they even thrive on unpredictability.

This book takes an individualized, flexible approach to organizing and can benefit anyone who applies the principles it sets forth. Those whose disorganization has a medical or complex emotional basis, however, should also seek professional attention to get at the root of the disorder.

Help for Attention Deficit Disorder

Einstein, Edison, and Mozart probably had what today is known as *attention deficit disorder,* or *ADD*. ADD is a medical condition that can impair the functioning and overall well-being of children and adults. Sufferers demonstrate some combination of impulsivity, procrastination, inattention, distractibility, restlessness, social inappropriateness, and underachievement. If you suspect that you have or someone close to you has ADD, it's important to consult a health professional.

For the person with ADD, getting and staying organized are like trying to operate a flashlight with the batteries in upside down. Those with ADD fall short of their goals because they have difficulty planning and staying with a project. Because they often leave tasks unfinished, they fail to realize a sense of accomplishment. Problems seem unsolvable, and even the smallest responsibilities are huge burdens. Many ADD children and adults benefit from medication, counseling, technological devices, and organizing techniques. Professional organizers often work wonders with people who have ADD. Learning how to simplify complex tasks makes projects achievable. Hidden talents appear, creativity blossoms, and self-esteem is restored.

Two doctors who have written about attention deficit disorder suggest that for those suffering with ADD, "organization is everything."[3] Although organization is not *quite* "everything," becoming organized can be a great help to someone with ADD. Organization, however, is not a substitute for proper medical attention.

Help for Chronic Disorganization

You may have never heard of chronic disorganization, but you may know someone who is affected by it. *Chronic disorganization (CD)* is disorganization with a long history; it undermines a person's ability to think, relax, and work and lessens one's quality of life, every day, day in and day out, for decades.[4] As already mentioned, the ability to organize not only involves how people process information, but also is tied to their emotions, cultures, and environments.[5] That's why a strategy that clicks with a logical thinker might backfire with a more creative type, for whom conventional time-management, filing, and storage systems can be very frustrating. Chronically disorganized people have usually tried the traditional approaches. Working with or learning from specialists who have researched CD, however, can be a turning point.

The National Study Group on Chronic Disorganization (NSGCD), for which author Judith Kohlberg is a leading researcher, is helping those with chronic disorganization.

The following books can help you learn more about CD and how to deal with it:

Kolberg, Judith and FileHeads Professional Organizers. *What Every Professional Organizer Needs to Know about Chronic Disorganization*, 1998.

Kolberg, Judith. *Conquering Chronic Disorganization*. Squall Press, Inc., Decatur, GA, 1999.

Lehmkuhl, Dorothy and Dolores Cotter Lamping, C.S.W. *Organizing for the Creative Person*. Crown Trade Paperbacks, New York, New York, 1994.

Before You Organize...Prioritize

The purpose of organizing is to put your *life* in order, not to put your *things* in order. You must determine what's really important to you and be honest with yourself about values and principles.

Step 1: Determine Your Principles

What are principles? Principles are your personal ideals; they guide your conduct in every aspect of your life and apply to all your circumstances and activities. They are the intangible concepts that you value—even though you can't see them, buy them, or touch them—such as honesty, fairness, growth, equality, independence, integrity, loyalty, order, stability, peace, beauty, unity, friendship, intelligence, love, and service.

Why should you determine your principles? Because they govern your thoughts and actions. When your principles are clear in your mind, you can develop workable priorities, responsibilities, goals, and objectives; choose activities purposefully; and make decisions confidently. Ultimately, to know your principles is to know yourself.

activities

objectives

goals

priorities

principles

"Things which matter most must never be at the mercy of things which matter least."

–Goethe

As the pyramid suggests, your principles govern your daily activities through the hierarchy of priorities, goals, objectives, and activities. When your principles are unsteady, the weakness is magnified at every level: Priorities are unsound, goals are shaky, objectives are indistinct, and activities are chaotic.

How do you determine your principles? Some of you may already know what you value most. Others may want to think carefully about it. When you have found yourself saying, "It's the principle of the thing," was it when an antique dealer misrepresented the value of that violin you bought? ("It's not the money I spent, it's the dishonesty....") Or when a colleague took all the credit for a project when you did most of the work? ("It's just not fair!") Or when you reported all your cash income, even the garage-sale profits, on your tax return? ("My integrity is worth more than 40 or 50 bucks.")

Think about what gives you the deepest satisfaction; what makes you feel uncomfortable or guilty; what you most admire in others; what kind of people you want your children to be. Reflecting on these things will give you clues to values and principles you might not be aware of.

Defining what is most important to you can require a lot of soul-searching. Although you might not be able to do a thorough examination of your principles in a few hours or days, at least a preliminary effort is an essential first step to becoming truly organized. It might help you to discuss your values with someone who knows you well and will be honest with you.

Now it's time to complete step 1: On the Principles and Priorities Worksheet in the following section, list in column 1 the principles or values that are the most important to you. These will become the foundation on which you'll build your priorities, goals, objectives, and finally your activities.

Step 2: Determine Priorities

Why establish priorities? Most people are too busy to do everything they have to do, ought to do, and want to do. Priorities help you decide what needs to be done first, most often, or not at all. Effectively prioritizing ensures that you'll fulfill the obligations over which you have no control, such as paying taxes and taking care of financial and legal matters; give appropriate attention to other responsibilities; and assess the benefits of activities, discarding or refusing the ones that don't adequately support your principles. You learn to find better, easier ways to do things. You learn to recognize who and how many will benefit from an activity.

Time Is Money

Time is money; managing your time is, in turn, managing your money. "People who are paid by the hour are much more aware of the value of time than are salaried workers. (If you don't believe this, try getting a psychiatrist or a plumber to take an hour off during the day to discuss some minor matter.)"[6]

Priorities clarify your goals, objectives, and activities. You can devote most of your time, energy, and money to the people and ideals most important to you instead of loading your resources onto a vessel that is going in the wrong direction. Take your time when sorting out your priorities. Consider discussing them with a good friend or with family members.

Your "Hourly Rate"

*For purposes of time management—an important component of organiza-
tion—consider yourself paid by the hour. To find your rate, take your annual
salary (or what you think you're worth), divide by two, and knock off those
zeroes. What's left is your hourly "wage." Say you're earning or could earn
$100,000 a year. Half of that is $50,000. Omit the three zeroes and you
have your rate: $50 an hour. WOW!*

And when you're considering how you want to spend your time,

Remember,
The more stuff you have…
The more you have to worry about,
The more you have to clean,
The more you have to repair,
The more you have to store,
The more you have to dust,
The more you have to work,
The more you have to have!
And, if you ever move…

You already filled out column 1 of the following chart in step 1. To accomplish
step 2, in column 2, list *related* areas of your life that are important to you. If
growth is one of your principles, education and spirituality may be important to
you. These are the *priorities* in your life at this time. Some will apply to more than
one value or principle. For example:

Column 1: Principles	Column 2: Priorities
1. Beauty	Home decorating
2. Growth	Education, spirituality
3. Service	Volunteering
4. Love	Spouse, children
5. Independence	Finances
6. Order	Home decorating, finances

Here are a few examples of priorities and what they might involve:

- ▲ Personal growth: spiritual and emotional well-being
- ▲ Children: health, education, well-being
- ▲ Health: stamina, nutrition
- ▲ Financial security: budget, investments, insurance
- ▲ Professional development: training
- ▲ Grooming: wardrobe, hairstyle
- ▲ Meals: plans, recipes
- ▲ School and education: homework, reading

- ▲ Friendships: social occasions
- ▲ Cultural growth: concerts, music lessons
- ▲ Pets: grooming, licenses, shots, and medicines
- ▲ Clothing: laundry, sewing, mending
- ▲ Cars: repair, upkeep
- ▲ Volunteering: Scouts, Habitat for Humanity, Red Cross
- ▲ Household: decoration, appliances

Principles and Priorities Worksheet

Column 1: Principles	Column 2: Priorities	Percent
1. _____	_____	_____
2. _____	_____	_____
3. _____	_____	_____
4. _____	_____	_____
5. _____	_____	_____
6. _____	_____	_____
7. _____	_____	_____
8. _____	_____	_____
9. _____	_____	_____
10. _____	_____	_____

Review column 2 on your Principles and Priorities Worksheet. Perhaps you listed health, family, spiritual beliefs, friendships, personal growth, career, grooming, and finances. (Sometimes a principle and a priority can be the same.) Are there important areas of your life missing from column 2? Add them to the list if they represent valued principles. If not, reexamine how important they really are.

Work on your Principles and Priorities Worksheet. After revising your Principles and Priorities lists, if necessary, start a separate worksheet for each priority. You can use the Priority Worksheet forms on the following pages. For now, just name each priority on the top line. In subsequent steps, you will complete the goals, objectives, and activities.

Sample Priority Worksheet

Priority/responsibility: _____ _Health_ _____

Goal: *(Goals and objectives are covered in step 4)* _____

   Objective: _____

      Activities: *(Activities are covered in step 5)* _____

      _____

   Objective: _____

      Activities: _____

      _____

Goal: _____

   Objective: _____

      Activities: _____

      _____

   Objective: _____

      Activities: _____

      _____

Priority Worksheet #1

Priority/responsibility: _____

_____

Goal: _____

_____

Objective: _____

_____

Activities: _____

_____

Objective: _____

_____

Activities: _____

_____

Goal: _____

_____

Objective: _____

_____

Activities: _____

_____

Objective: _____

_____

Activities: _____

_____

Priority Worksheet #2

Priority/responsibility: _____

_____

Goal: _____

_____

Objective: _____

_____

Activities: _____

_____

Objective: _____

_____

Activities: _____

_____

Goal: _____

_____

Objective: _____

_____

Activities: _____

_____

Objective: _____

_____

Activities: _____

_____

Priority Worksheet #3

Priority/responsibility: _____

_____

Goal: _____

_____

Objective: _____

_____

Activities: _____

_____

Objective: _____

_____

Activities: _____

_____

Goal: _____

_____

Objective: _____

_____

Activities: _____

_____

Objective: _____

_____

Activities: _____

_____

Priority Worksheet #4

Priority/responsibility: _____

_____

Goal: _____

Objective: _____

Activities: _____

Objective: _____

Activities: _____

Goal: _____

Objective: _____

Activities: _____

Objective: _____

Activities: _____

Priority Worksheet #5

Priority/responsibility: _____

_____

Goal: _____

_____

   Objective: _____

_____

      Activities: _____

_____

   Objective: _____

_____

      Activities: _____

_____

Goal: _____

_____

   Objective: _____

_____

      Activities: _____

_____

   Objective: _____

_____

      Activities: _____

_____

Priority Worksheet #6

Priority/responsibility: _____

_____

Goal: _____

_____

　　Objective: _____

_____

　　　　Activities: _____

_____

　　Objective: _____

_____

　　　　Activities: _____

_____

Goal: _____

_____

　　Objective: _____

_____

　　　　Activities: _____

_____

　　Objective: _____

_____

　　　　Activities: _____

_____

Priority Worksheet #7

Priority/responsibility: _____

_____

Goal: _____

_____

    Objective: _____

_____

        Activities: _____

_____

    Objective: _____

_____

        Activities: _____

_____

Goal: _____

_____

    Objective: _____

_____

        Activities: _____

_____

    Objective: _____

_____

        Activities: _____

_____

Priority Worksheet #8

Priority/responsibility: _____

_____

Goal: _____

_____

Objective: _____

_____

Activities: _____

_____

Objective: _____

_____

Activities: _____

_____

Goal: _____

_____

Objective: _____

_____

Activities: _____

_____

Objective: _____

_____

Activities: _____

_____

Priority Worksheet #9

Priority/responsibility: _____

_____

Goal: _____

_____

Objective: _____

_____

Activities: _____

_____

Objective: _____

_____

Activities: _____

_____

Goal: _____

_____

Objective: _____

_____

Activities: _____

_____

Objective: _____

_____

Activities: _____

_____

Priority Worksheet #10

Priority/responsibility: _____

_____

Goal: _____

_____

Objective: _____

_____

Activities: _____

_____

Objective: _____

_____

Activities: _____

_____

Goal: _____

_____

Objective: _____

_____

Activities: _____

_____

Objective: _____

_____

Activities: _____

_____

Step 3: Log Your Time

Now that you've clarified what's important to you, it might be interesting to see where your time goes and how well your activities reflect your priorities. Why not log your time for a week or two to find out? Record everything you do alongside the related priority. If you take a nap, write "rested for an hour" and the priority it serves–for example, "take good care of myself." If another priority is "spend time with my children," that's probably what you would write next to "read a story to Jack and Eli."

You might discover that some of your time is unrelated to or even sabotaging your priorities. Maybe someone talked you into spending three hours canvassing your neighborhood for a candidate you've never heard of; or your chatty sister-in-law kept you on the phone so long you missed the bus to work. In the Priority column, you could write "none," or you could write the priority that was sabotaged and put an X or line through it, like this:

7:30–8:15 a.m. on the phone with Maggie ~~career~~

On the other hand, you could find that something has become important to you without your knowing it. If that's the case, revisit your Principles and Priorities Worksheet.

When you log your time during a relatively normal week, your attention to principles and priorities comes into focus. Are you "putting your time where your mouth is?" There are some things you may not be able to change; but there are many things you can.

Here's an example of a completed time log that you can use to help you get started with your own time log.

Sample Time Log

Day	Time	Activity	Priority
11/2	6:00 a.m.	Shower, wash hair	grooming
	6:30 a.m.	Get dressed	grooming
	7:00 a.m.	Fix breakfast for kids	children
	7:30 a.m.	Help kids with project	children
	8:00 a.m.	" "	children
	8:30 a.m.	Plan 10 nutritious meals	health—all
	9:00 a.m.	" "	health—all
	9:30 a.m.	Jog	health—me
	10:00 a.m.	" "	health—me
	10:30 a.m.	Read paper	education

Time Log

Day	Time	Activity	Priority
_____	6:00 a.m.	_____	_____
	6:30 a.m.	_____	_____
	7:00 a.m.	_____	_____
	7:30 a.m.	_____	_____
	8:00 a.m.	_____	_____
	8:30 a.m.	_____	_____
	9:00 a.m.	_____	_____
	9:30 a.m.	_____	_____

Day	Time	Activity	Priority
	10:00 a.m.	_____	_____
	10:30 a.m.	_____	_____
	11:00 a.m.	_____	_____
	11:30 a.m.	_____	_____
	12:00 p.m.	_____	_____
	12:30 p.m.	_____	_____
	1:00 p.m.	_____	_____
	1:30 p.m.	_____	_____
	2:00 p.m.	_____	_____
	2:30 p.m.	_____	_____
	3:00 p.m.	_____	_____
	3:30 p.m.	_____	_____
	4:00 p.m.	_____	_____
	4:30 p.m.	_____	_____
	5:00 p.m.	_____	_____
	5:30 p.m.	_____	_____
	6:00 p.m.	_____	_____
	6:30 p.m.	_____	_____
	7:00 p.m.	_____	_____
	7:30 p.m.	_____	_____
	8:00 p.m.	_____	_____
	8:30 p.m.	_____	_____
	9:00 p.m.	_____	_____
	9:30 p.m.	_____	_____

(continues)

(continued)

Day	Time	Activity	Priority
	10:00 p.m.	_____	_____
	10:30 p.m.	_____	_____
	11:00 p.m.	_____	_____
	11:30 p.m.	_____	_____

Notes about time spent:

_____

_____

_____

_____

_____

_____

_____

_____

Calculate the percentage of time you spent on each activity and priority. See how well your activities supported your priorities. You may find that you spent 5 percent on hobbies/leisure, 10 percent on clothing care, 5 percent on meal preparation, 40 percent sleeping, 30 percent on career, 10 percent going door-to-door for the mystery candidate, and so on.

Are important priorities missing altogether? Do your priorities actually determine how you spend your time, or did you fail to "plan nutritious meals" because you were tramping around the neighborhood handing out campaign flyers? Go back to your Principles and Priorities Worksheet and put the approximate percentages of time you spent on each in the Percent column.

How Well Do You Spend Your Time?

You used the Time Log to determine how you spend your time. You can ascertain how *well* you spend your time by answering these questions:

1. Do you follow through on tasks until they are completed?

    ❏ Yes   ❏ No

2. Are you able to focus on one activity for a long period of time?

    ❏ Yes   ❏ No

3. Are you enjoying most of the things you do?

    ❏ Yes   ❏ No

4. Do you spend enough time on a task so you can enjoy it without having to hurry through it?

    ❏ Yes   ❏ No

5. Are you efficient without being ineffective?

    ❏ Yes   ❏ No

6. Are you doing things you like to do?

    ❏ Yes   ❏ No

7. Are you delegating or refusing to do tasks that others could or should do?

    ❏ Yes   ❏ No

8. Are most of your activities either necessary or enjoyable?

    ❏ Yes   ❏ No

9. Do you plan enough time for a task so you can do it well?

    ❏ Yes   ❏ No

10. Do you plan breaks for yourself so you don't get burned out?

    ❏ Yes   ❏ No

Any "no" answers signal areas you can work on to become both more effective and more satisfied.

Step 4: Determine Your Goals and Objectives

"To begin with the end in mind means to start with a clear understanding of your destination."

–Stephen R. Covey

For each priority, decide roughly how much time you want to or can realistically devote, then determine a goal or goals to go with it. Goals are long-range promises to yourself. They are more tangible than priorities and principles. "An effective goal focuses primarily on results rather than activity."[7] An objective, then, is a strategy or more immediate plan for meeting a goal. Goals are measurable accomplishments, destinations you can reach through a series of plans (objectives) and steps (activities).

Both goals and objectives carry with them specific requirements and objectives. When setting goals and objectives, remember to make them realistic but yet somewhat demanding. If you know you won't do something, don't set it as a goal or objective. On the other hand, the goals and objectives shouldn't be too easy; make yourself reach a little. Avoid setting simultaneous goals that conflict or that aren't compatible, like quitting smoking and losing 30 pounds. Goals and objectives should be measurable, with beginning and ending dates.

Give Your Goals and Objectives the SMART Test

Make your goal a promise to yourself—a resolution. A goal is a target that helps direct your objective. In the words of the great philosopher Yogi Berra, "If you don't know where you're going, you might wind up somewhere else." If Benson High's goal is to win a football game against Central High, one of Benson's objectives might be to cross Central's goal line often. Is that a good objective for Benson?

Not really; it doesn't pass the SMART test. SMART goals and objectives are Specific, Measurable, Achievable, Rewarding, *and* Timed. *If your goal is financial security by the end of next year, one objective may be "to put $10,000 in a savings account by December 31 of this year." This objective meets the SMART test; it is*

▲ **Specific:** *It includes details ("put* $10,000 *into a savings account").*

▲ **Measurable:** *You'll not only know whether or not you achieve the goal or objective, you'll know exactly how far you fell short of or surpassed it.*

▲ **Achievable:** *It is possible for you to accomplish this goal.*

▲ **Rewarding:** *You'll feel good about being closer to your objective and you'll be more financially secure.*

▲ **Timed:** *The goal has a deadline: December 31.*

Now that you have a goal and objectives, you need to put wheels on it. Wheels are the ideas, steps, activities, and resources that are part of the planning process. To plan how to put $10,000 into a savings account by December 31, answer the following:

▲ What activities should you engage in? In what sequence?

▲ Who would be helpful to talk with?

▲ What obstacles might you encounter? How can you avoid these obstacles?

Now take it one step at a time and you'll cross your goal line. In pursuing your goal, keep in mind that "big things happen when you do the little things right."[8]

If your priority is your health and a goal is achieving your ideal weight, you may need to plan a sensible diet, to visit your doctor, and to begin an exercise program. A specific objective might be, "Walk for 40 minutes three times a week starting next week and continuing through May 1." Another might be, "Plan 30 nutritious, appetizing meals by November 15."

If your priority is your home and a goal is to keep the structure in good repair, you might have to plan for painting, caulking, plumbing, and electrical work. Your objective might include hiring an electrician by April 1 and painting the upstairs bedrooms by the last day of school.

Whatever your goals might be, develop requirements and objectives for each one and write them on your Priority Worksheets. As you plan, visualize the process and the outcome of each objective; determine where you are right now relative to each objective; and decide what has to happen for you to reach it. The process you visualize should feel somewhat challenging. But if you break into a cold sweat just thinking about it, revise your expectations downward a bit.

For example, a specific goal for keeping your home in good repair might be to redecorate your kitchen. Picture how your kitchen looks now; let's call that "picture A." Visualize how you want the kitchen to look after it is redecorated–"picture B." With these two pictures in mind, imagine what steps you'll have to take to get from "picture A" to "picture B."

Step 5: Determine Your Activities

Now it's time to act. Decide what activities are necessary to carry out each objective and goal, based on your priorities and founded on your principles. (Remember those?)

Factors in your planning are

- ▲ Time
- ▲ Money and other material resources
- ▲ Steps to take (action)

If one of your objectives is to build five birdhouses in three months, arrange your activities so that you're not spending more time driving around town looking for nails and wood than you are in actual construction. (Don't waste time; those birds are depending on you.)

When scheduling activities, ask yourself lots of questions:

▲ Does this conflict with steps toward other goals and objectives?

▲ Do I want to spend that much time?

▲ Is there a more efficient process?

▲ What habits should be changed or dropped? (Sometimes we just get into ruts and do things without giving them much thought.)

▲ Am I properly focused?

Now go back and list your activities on your Priority Worksheets. After you've listed your activities on your Priority Worksheets, chapter 2 will help you plan the order in which you should perform them.

Checklist: What You Learned

This chapter showed you how to do the following things:

❏ List your principles.
❏ Determine your priorities.
❏ Log your time for one or two weeks.
❏ Analyze your use of time.
❏ Set and list goals for your priorities.
❏ Set and list objectives for goals and apply the SMART test.
❏ List activities to help you accomplish your objectives.

Now that you have completed these steps, chapter 2 will show you how to record when and how often to carry out the activities you've planned.

Plan to Meet Your Goals

"...At the heart of time management is management of self."
–R. Alec MacKenzie[1]

You probably will do steps 1, 2, and 3–explained in chapter 1–only one time. You may add to or subtract from them occasionally, but for the most part your principles, priorities, and time usage will remain as they are. Your goals, which you determined in step 4, may change occasionally, and your objectives will change more often. Examine them monthly to see whether you are on track. Your activities, which you listed in step 5, may change even more often.

Steps 6, 7, and 8 of the prioritization process, which we will tackle in this chapter, need to be done annually and when there are significant changes in your life–marriage, a new baby, a death in the family, a new job or house, a child leaving home, or perhaps just a change of mind.

Setting Agendas

In this chapter, you will continue the steps toward prioritizing your life, a process that puts you on the path to organization. You'll learn to

▲ Record the activities necessary for accomplishing goals and objectives.

▲ Set up annual, monthly, and weekly lists of activities.

▲ Plan ahead and stay on top of priority activities.

Step 6: Set Up an Annual Agenda

For this step, refer to your Priority Worksheets from step 2 in chapter 1. You will create an Annual Agenda that includes, for each priority, all the activities that you want or need to accomplish once or several times per year, but less often than monthly. Examples of these types of activities include

- ▲ Income tax due date
- ▲ Dentist appointments
- ▲ School vacations
- ▲ Holidays, birthdays
- ▲ Graduation days
- ▲ Automobile oil changes
- ▲ Furnace inspections
- ▲ Changing furnace filters
- ▲ Planting tulip bulbs
- ▲ Termite inspection

Be complete and thorough. It's important to consider each priority carefully so you don't miss something important. In most cases, you don't need to list the actual date of an activity; just write it under the appropriate month. Check with other family members to make sure you include everybody's (important) activities.

Your Annual Agenda will give you a good overview of the year. You'll discover how much you actually do in a year, month by month. It may discourage you from taking on new projects or encourage you to drop other activities so you can devote your time to what's important to you.

Use the Annual Agenda to schedule vacations and large projects. You may decide to get all of the family's health checkups out of the way in April or complete your Christmas shopping in November. There is much we don't know ahead of time and much we can't control. You need to take responsibility for what you can foresee and schedule accordingly.

For each activity you plan, see which one of these statements applies:

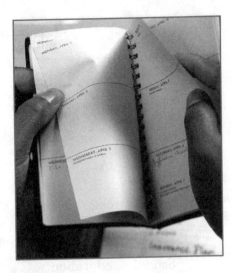

▲ I have to or must do it.

▲ I should do it.

▲ It would be nice if I did it.

▲ I really don't have to do it at all.

Regarding the car, for example:

▲ **I must:** Get license, pay taxes, get insurance, make payments, put the title in a safe place, know how to change the tires, have regular tune-ups.

▲ **I should:** Equip it with flashlight, jumper cables, and a jack; read the manual; rotate the tires; have it waxed.

▲ **It would be nice if I:** Installed a sunroof.

▲ **I really don't have to:** Scrub the carpet with a toothbrush.

The *have-to's*, or *musts*, need to be done or planned before the *shoulds* and the *would-be-nices*.

The chart on the following page lists some sample priorities with related activities.

Sample Priorities and Activities

Priorities	Activities
Health:	Doctor and dentist appointments–April, October
Financial:	Set up savings account–January; income tax–April; reassess investments–June
Job or career:	Training course–September, October
Grooming:	Get a permanent–February
School or education:	Spring vacation–March; summer vacation–May 15 to August 15
Special friends and events:	Holiday cards–December
Pets:	Shots–June; license–March
Clothing:	Hire wardrobe coordinator–March; store winter clothes–May
Cars:	Have car repainted–April; tune-up–July
Volunteer activities:	Project due–November
Household business:	Termite inspection–October; storm windows–October, April; piano tuned–June
Children:	shop for school clothes, August
Spouse:	Second honeymoon–September

Sample Annual Agenda

	HEALTH	$$$	CHILDREN	SPOUSE	FRIENDS	CAREER	EDUCATION	VOLUNTEER	HOUSE	GROOMING	CLOTHING	CARS	PETS	OTHER
JANUARY														
FEBRUARY														
MARCH														
APRIL														
MAY														
JUNE														
JULY														
AUGUST														
SEPTEMBER														
OCTOBER														
NOVEMBER														
DECEMBER														

Sample Annual Agenda

	Health	$$$	Children	Spouse	Education
Jan		Shop after-Christmas sales			
Feb	dental appts.		room mother		appt. with counselor
Mar		income tax	spring break		
April	yearly exams				
May		plant garden		bed and breakfast	
June	eye appts.		graduation celebrations		summer class begins
July					
Aug	6-month dental checkups		family vacation		
Sept		garage sale			computer workshop
Oct				anniversary	
Nov	attend wellness class				
Dec			school vacation		

Annual Agenda

	Health	$$$	Children	Spouse	Education
Jan					
Feb					
Mar					
April					
May					
June					
July					
Aug					
Sept					
Oct					
Nov					
Dec					

Annual Agenda

	Health	$$$	Children	Spouse	Education
Jan					
Feb					
Mar					
April					
May					
June					
July					
Aug					
Sept					
Oct					
Nov					
Dec					

Annual Agenda

	Health	$$$	Children	Spouse	Education
Jan					
Feb					
Mar					
April					
May					
June					
July					
Aug					
Sept					
Oct					
Nov					
Dec					

Annual Agenda

	Health	$$$	Children	Spouse	Education
Jan					
Feb					
Mar					
April					
May					
June					
July					
Aug					
Sept					
Oct					
Nov					
Dec					

Too Pooped to Cook?

A growing small-business niche is dedicated to helping you manage your home and family. These providers usually charge less than their large-firm competitors (if there are any) because of lower overhead. Their services are worth exploring if you don't have the time, tools, or talent to do the jobs yourself. They include

- ▲ *Organizing storage, furniture, and time*
- ▲ *Preparing meals and delivering them to your home*
- ▲ *Scrapbooking*
- ▲ *Designing and installing closet systems*
- ▲ *Bill paying and checkbook reconciliation*
- ▲ *Running errands*
- ▲ *Personal shopping*
- ▲ *Gift buying, wrapping, and sending*
- ▲ *Transporting kids to and from school and activities*
- ▲ *Housekeeping*

Check the classifieds and the telephone directory, or call your local chamber of commerce for more suggestions.

Step 7: Set Up a Monthly Agenda

Looking over your priority list and using your Annual Agenda as a guide, write down what you need to do once or twice a month, along with the week in which you want to do it. For example, you may want to have your hair cut the first week of each month and take care of correspondence the last week of every month. Other monthly or semimonthly responsibilities might include attending board meetings, paying bills, planning meals, catching up on mending and ironing, and so on.

Here are some items you might include on your Monthly Agenda:

Priorities	Activities
Health:	Plan nutritious menus for the month—first week
Financial:	Pay bills—first and third weeks; reconcile bank statement—fourth week
Job or career:	Staff meeting—first Monday
Grooming:	Haircut—second Tuesday
Meals:	Plan menus—first week
Spiritual and educational:	Parent meeting—fourth Thursday; church board—second Tuesday
Special friends/events:	Buy birthday cards—fourth week
Pets:	Wash and brush dogs—second week
Clothing:	Catch up on mending and ironing—first week
Cars:	Wash—first week
Volunteer activities:	Meetings, calling—third week
Household business:	Change furnace filter—first week
Children:	Take for haircuts—second week
Spouse:	Have special night out—third week

Sample Monthly Agenda

Priorities

	1. Health	2. Financial	3. Career	4. Grooming	5. Education
1st Week	plan menus for the month	pay bills	staff meeting		
2nd Week				haircut	church board
3rd Week		pay bills			
4th Week					parent meeting

Monthly Agenda

Priorities

	1.	2.	3.	4.	5.
1st Week					
2nd Week					
3rd Week					
4th Week					

Monthly Agenda

Priorities

	1.	2.	3.	4.	5.
1st Week					
2nd Week					
3rd Week					
4th Week					

Step 8: Set Up a Weekly Agenda

Referring once again to your priority list, use the Sample Weekly Agenda as a guide and write down the things you do (or need to do) every week. They may include giving yourself a manicure, watering plants, writing letters, washing clothes, cleaning, ironing, or running errands. You might want to do all your weekly tasks in one day or give yourself a free day to sleep or read or paint. Knowing that you have a whole day for yourself can make the rest of the week go more smoothly. Here are some ideas:

Priorities	Activities
Health:	Aerobics–Monday, Wednesday, Friday
Financial:	Bank deposit–Monday
Job or career:	Communication course–Tuesday evening
Grooming:	Manicure–Friday
Meals:	Food shopping–Tuesday
School or education:	Class–Tuesday evening
Relatives/special friends/events:	Call parents–Sunday
Pets:	Bath–Saturday (summer)
Clothing:	Laundry–Monday, Friday; dry cleaner–Monday
Cars:	Fill with gasoline; wash–Saturday
Volunteer activities:	ABC meeting–Friday, 9 a.m.
Household business:	Correspondence–Saturday
Children:	Coach softball–Wednesday evening
Spouse:	Go to movie with–Friday evening

Sample Weekly Agenda

Priorities

	1. Health	2. Financial	3. Career	4. Grooming	5. Education
Mon	aerobics	bank deposit			
Tues	class				communica-tion course
Wed	aerobics				
Thurs					
Fri	aerobics			manicure	
Sat					
Sun					

Weekly Agenda

Priorities

	1.	2.	3.	4.	5.
Mon					
Tues					
Wed					
Thurs					
Fri					
Sat					
Sun					

Weekly Agenda

Priorities

	6.	7.	8.	9.	10.
Mon					
Tues					
Wed					
Thurs					
Fri					
Sat					
Sun					

Using Your Agendas

You should set up your Annual Agenda once and amend it as needed throughout the year. Revise it at the end of the year; the last week in December is a good time. Unless there have been big changes in your life, much will remain the same. Even so, take some time to rethink your priorities and responsibilities, reassess your needs, and review your circumstances. Write in new items; delete obsolete ones.

After designing your Annual Agenda, make appointments that must be arranged months in advance.

At the end of each month, check your Annual Agenda for the next six weeks and transfer relevant activities–including those from social, business, school, church, and other schedules–onto your planner. Make necessary appointments for hair-cuts, repairs, lessons, and so forth. Reschedule if you have conflicts. Note birth-days, anniversaries, and other important occasions. Write down in your planner what days you need to buy gifts and when to mail cards.

At the end of each week (on Sunday night, for example), spend 20 minutes taking stock of the upcoming 10 days to two weeks. Add specifics from your Monthly Agenda. Make it part of your routine to look at your planner, see what you have coming up, and prepare for it. Know in advance that you need to have a dress hemmed or a suit coat cleaned to wear to a wedding, or that it's time to buy a gift for an upcoming shower.

Write down the errands you have to do in the week ahead and decide when to do them. Set aside time to do laundry, send greeting cards, balance your checkbook, clean the house, have a manicure, and catch up on your weekly responsibilities. Remind yourself of car-pool assignments, lessons, or trash pick-up times.

Every night, look over your schedule for the next day. Reschedule activities you planned but didn't complete. Plan your errands and projects for the next day. In chapter 3, you will discover tools for day-to-day time management including simplifying errands, list-making, and time-saving techniques.

You now have sketched your big picture and have listed some activities such as "plant bulbs in October," "write letters the first week of the month," or "take out trash on Tuesdays," on your agenda. You may have written specific times on your planner, such as "Katy's dentist appointment, 11 a.m., November 19" or "Evan's graduation, 2 p.m., May 15."

Checklist: What You Learned

This chapter showed you how to do the following things:

❏ Write activities for each priority on an Annual Agenda.
❏ Write activities for each priority on a Monthly Agenda.
❏ Write activities for each priority on a Weekly Agenda.
❏ Write specific dates of which you are currently aware in your planner.

Chapter 3

Day-to-Day Time Management

"Budget your time like you were paying for it...because you are...."

–Donna Goldfein[10]

Unlike chapters 2 and 3, this chapter does not have steps. Instead, it teaches skills and gives suggestions for how to become a better day-to-day time manager. In this chapter, you will learn to

▲ Be proficient at using a planner (I use the term *planner* to refer to a calendar or planner.)

▲ Use to-do lists effectively

▲ Overcome procrastination...today

▲ Make better use of your time

Daily Organization with a Planner

Your planner may be an 8½ × 11 notebook or a smaller version. As mentioned in chapter 2, find the type of planner that best suits your needs. Whatever you choose, have just one planner for your day-to-day use. If you have an additional planner for your job, resist the temptation to put work-related commitments on your home planner unless they occur outside normal working hours–such as an evening meeting, for example, or a convention in the Bahamas. Likewise, in your work planner, add home items only if they occur during work hours. Examples might include a child's softball tournament or an appointment with the doctor.

Ideally, however, you should try not to have more than one planner.

Now that you have listed priorities, goals, and objectives, and written your annual, monthly, and weekly responsibilities in your agenda sheets, you are ready to use your planner.

Before scheduling new appointments, create times each week to do something relaxing and rejuvenating. Keep in mind the simple pleasures–a walk in the park, a visit to the zoo, or reading your favorite childhood book. Write these "dates with yourself" in your planner and keep the commitments!

Selecting a Planner

Before you go shopping for planners, know your options. Do you want a "tabbed, daily, dated, unlined planner," a "week-in-view, undated, lined, loose-leaf planner," or another of the hundreds of possible combinations? You can find planning pads and notebooks in office-supply and stationery stores, on the Internet, and in catalogs. Consider your requirements:

▲ *Appearance. Do you want real leather or faux leather binding? Black, brown, or red?*

▲ *Flexibility. Spiral binding makes for a more compact planner, although spiral-bound planners are neither refillable nor flexible.*

▲ *Format. There are pocket, purse, and briefcase sizes, generally ranging from 3 × 5 to 9 × 12 inches.*

▲ *Extras. Some planners come with additional and sometimes mystifying features, such as tabbed A–Z telephone/address directories, notepads, project planning pages, time-zone and area-code maps, and many others. If you can't think of a way to use them, take them out.*

Whatever you choose, use it to get stuff out of your head and onto the page!

When scheduling your activities, remember to use your prime time (or high productivity time) wisely. *Prime time* is the time of day when you are most alert, have lots of energy, and can concentrate best. Sensible use of your prime time is a key to organizing your day and week efficiently. Use this time for work that requires creativity or concentration. Also, find a place where you are apt to be free from distractions. You will accomplish much more in less time.

Using Your Planner for Things Other Than Appointments

Planners can be useful in many ways other than just recording appointments:

▲ When you need to call someone, put his or her name and phone number in the planner on the date you need to call. That way you don't need to look up the phone number if you need to cancel an appointment or call for directions.

▲ If you are going to a party and you are not familiar with the location, write not only the time of the party but also the address. Other entries for your planner can include things you need to take with you to the party, such as gifts or borrowed items.

▲ When you receive schedules for club events, meetings, and soccer games, write the dates and locations in your planner.

▲ For birthday, anniversary, or other greeting cards, note in your planner the day you should buy the card and the day you should mail it.

▲ Use your planner for backward planning. If you promised to build a tree house by September 1, write down a target date. Give yourself plenty of time and allow for mistakes and emergencies. If your target date is August 15, plan to have it ready to paint by August 10, nailed together by August 5, all supplies purchased by July 25, and "architectural renderings" ready by July 15. Write each step and goal in your planner.

▲ Use your planner to set deadlines for yourself.

▲ If you have a large project or major task, break it up into smaller tasks, each with its own deadline. You'll feel a sense of satisfaction after you complete each step and draw nearer to the project's finish.

Five Great Preventive Measures That Save Time

1. ***Think before you buy.*** *Ask yourself some questions. Will your purchase last as long as it takes to pay for it? What maintenance does it require? Does that shirt require hand laundering? Do you already have an extension cord (maybe even six or seven) that's not being used? Will these curtains require a lot of time for upkeep? How good will this look in a year? Remember, every item you own takes time, space, effort, and attention.*

2. ***Stop, look, and listen before you say "yes" to added responsibilities.*** *We often say yes automatically when we're asked to carry out a task, join a group, or be on a committee. But before you say yes the next time your skills and wisdom are requested, ask yourself some good questions and then answer them:*

   ▲ *Which of my priorities does this honor?*

   ▲ *What is the time frame or deadline? (a week, two months, eternity?)*

   ▲ *What type of work or skill is required of me?*

   ▲ *Why did they ask me; why not, say, Martha Stewart?*

   ▲ *What is the purpose of the activity or committee?*

   ▲ *What specific days and times must I commit? How many meetings will there be?*

   ▲ *Whom will I work with?*

   Look at your other commitments, weigh the answers to these questions, and be aware of the level of dedication you usually give in such situations. Most important, give yourself a week to decide…then say yes (or no) with conviction.

---

3. ***Set up a home communication center.*** *Prevent scheduling nightmares by putting a family calendar for all activities and a bulletin board in a spot where all household members will bump into it—try the back hall or the kitchen. Pin phone lists and schedules on the bulletin board. Assign each person a color, and color-code activities and appointments. The 15 minutes you spend now creating the center will save hours and avert confusion later. This concept is addressed more fully in chapter 7.*

4. ***Create kits for saving time.*** *It takes only 10 or 15 minutes to create a kit that could save you 30 minutes and a lot of stress every time you use it. Kits entail simply having all your "tools" in a manageable container. Some ideas are*

   ▲ *Package-wrapping kit*

   ▲ *Bill-paying kit*

   ▲ *Correspondence kit*

   If you have enough space, create stations as well as kits. Stations are areas designated for specific tasks. You might want a station in your kitchen for making school lunches and one for taking care of pets. Kits and stations are especially helpful for tasks you find unpleasant or particularly messy.

5. ***Make a* to-don't *list.*** *Take inventory! Are your activities and tasks consistent with your values and well-being, or are they draining your energy? Be intentional about what you don't do. Make a to-don't list of things you do because you…*

   ▲ *Feel guilty*

   ▲ *Think you're supposed to*

   ▲ *Always have*

   ▲ *Have been flattered into doing it*

   ▲ *Can't say no*

   ▲ *Accept another's crisis as your own*

   ▲ *Think no one else can do it as well as or better than you*

   With all your to-don'ts, do make time for a handball game or a bubble bath!

Making Errands Easier

Does it seem as if you always have errands to run? Get in control by planning and creating some good systems and helpful habits.

▲ If you have lots to do, even after you act on your *to-don't* list, prioritize your errands. Delegate to others if possible. Leave plenty of time for the errands and activities you must do.

▲ When planning an errand, ask yourself whether someone else can do it on the way home from work or school.

▲ Use the phone or computer. Call ahead so you don't waste a lot of time going from place to place with no success. Also, remember that almost anything can be ordered by phone or online.

▲ Allow plenty of time. Plan for rush-hour traffic, busy salespeople, and the inability to find what you want.

▲ If you have many errands and they don't need to be done immediately, arrange them by geographic areas for different days. If you have a dentist appointment in the west end of the city, do all your "west end" errands that day.

▲ List your errands in order by making a mental map of the locations and planning accordingly. This way you won't be backtracking. On your list, include everything you have to take with you: checks to be deposited, coupons, clothes to be hemmed, library books to be returned, and so on.

▲ Designate a place in your house for things you need to take someplace—library books, store coupons, borrowed items, clothes for dry cleaning, and returnable bottles—or put them in your car ahead of time.

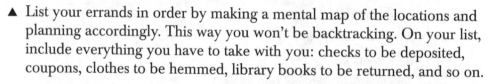

▲ Your wallet is a good place to save receipts and stubs needed for picking up items such as dry cleaning, photos, and shoes being repaired. Note in your planner the date and time they are to be ready.

▲ Consolidate errands; do as many in one day as possible. (You might have designated a particular day for errands on your Monthly or Weekly Agenda.)

▲ Take something to do when you think you might have to wait. Reading a good book, mending, balancing your checkbook, planning menus, or designing architectural renderings for your birdhouses will allow you to wait more patiently and accomplish something, too.

▲ When you are going to buy a gift, take the recipient's address with you so that the store can mail or deliver it for you. Know ahead of time which stores will gift-wrap, deliver, and mail packages.

▲ When you have lots to do, plan breaks and give yourself rewards.

▲ If you don't get a scheduled errand done, put it in the planner for the next or earliest possible day, or decide not to do it at all.

E-errands: Go Everywhere Without Leaving Home

by Mary Campbell, Columnist for Small Business Builder on ABCnews.com

Use your computer to save time and avoid frustration. Arm yourself with one of the many Internet directories or online-shopping guides (available in both the *Complete Idiot's Guide to...* and *...For Dummies* series) and enjoy the convenience and economy of this modern wonder. There are too many possibilities to list, but here are a few that are especially relevant to families and homes:

▲ **Organizing:** Go to www.NAPO.net and check out the National Association of Professional Organizers. There are other organizing Web sites, too. Enter "organizing" in a search engine (such as Yahoo!, Lycos, or Google) to get a list of the latest sites.

▲ **Data research:** Information about companies, people, geography, the economy, history, science, you name it. (In many areas, the Internet has much more data than the public library, though you won't want to tear up your library card just yet.)

▲ **Product research:** Consumer Reports online and hundreds of other agencies, companies, dedicated Web sites, and consumer forums, plus stores and manufacturers.

▲ **Price comparisons.**

▲ **Prescription orders and refills.**

▲ **Travel reservations, flight arrival and departure updates.**

▲ **Online phone and address books for personal and business use.** In addition, your e-mail address book likely allows you to enter not just names and mailboxes, but also birthdays, addresses, phone numbers, and much more.

▲ **Newspaper and magazine articles and clippings.**

▲ **Recipes.** You can even search by ingredient, so you'll know how to prepare all those leftover turnips.

▲ **Crafts and home-improvement projects, step by step.**

▲ **News, weather, road conditions,** television and movie schedules, things to do in your area, things to do where you're traveling.

▲ **Medical information,** including several sites that give you a possible diagnosis and tell you whether you need to see a doctor when you input symptoms.

▲ **Virtual "buddies" that guide you through and monitor your progress** in everything from losing weight and getting fit to quitting smoking, whether you're already in good shape or you have health problems such as heart disease, high blood pressure or cholesterol, diabetes, and so forth.

▲ **Planning systems and reminders.** These, available both as off-the-shelf software and online, even have pop-up windows that remind you when it's time to leave to pick up the kids.

▲ **Automatic delivery**–weekly, monthly, or at any other interval you prefer–of groceries, pet food, and other commodities (great if you keep running out of things because you didn't have time to shop), as well as prepared gourmet meals, locally grown organic produce, and office supplies.

▲ **Real estate searches** (by price, school district, size, age, condition, and other qualifications), virtual tours, mortgage comparisons, and applications.

▲ **Every other kind of shopping imaginable.** Many people report great success purchasing cars online, but you can also find out what you should be paying for any new or used car.

▲ **Banking.** From setting up and monitoring your account to transferring funds, investing in and tracking stocks and bonds, and paying your bills automatically.

▲ **Birthday cards** (many free and including animation and music) for postal or e-mail delivery. (Oh, and you can buy your stamps and look up ZIP codes, too.)

▲ **Web sites** (Set up your own, free!).

▲ **Classes.** Free tutorials or for-fee courses on hundreds of topics, credit courses from top universities, job-related skill training, and entire high-quality degree programs. (Many public and private schools have online modules allowing absent students to keep up with the class while they're sick or traveling.)

▲ **Music.** Compose it, download it, get CDs customized for yourself or as a gift.

▲ **Software.** Available on CD, usually inexpensively, for planting legumes, building a house, planning a wedding, playing bridge, managing your finances, doing your taxes, or learning Portuguese.

E-mail, too, can allow you to accomplish more in less time. You can have almost any kind of information update sent automatically: new specials at Eddie Bauer, new information on a health topic, low fares on airlines and destinations of your choice, or new tax regulations. Many Web sites are clearinghouses for e-mail tips; there's a time-management tip of the day; daily or weekly tips on computers, herbs and vitamins, grammar, online shopping, and healthy food; in fact there are thousands of free e-zines for every possible interest.

Your fax and e-mail can be ideal for making and confirming appointments, giving directions or instructions, issuing (informal) invitations, writing (informal) letters, contacting hard-to-reach or well-known people, contacting your elected representatives, and filing complaints.

Other telecommunication devices—handheld and laptop computers and wireless phones, for example—are invaluable if you're on the go a lot. The line is blurring between handheld computers and wireless phones, which are now available for accessing e-mail and the Internet as well as making and receiving calls. A laptop will do just about anything a desktop computer can. A handheld computer can store and retrieve information, translate between numerous languages, give you reminders, keep schedules and lists, and much, much more.

If you've put off getting a computer or another high-tech device, consider doing so now. Prices are unbelievably low, instruction is free or inexpensive (and you might not need any), and the possibilities for saving time and money are almost unlimited.

Much Ado About To-Do Lists

Used correctly and wisely, to-do lists reduce stress because they "remember" for you, plus they remind you of all you've accomplished. Get in the to-do-list habit.

▲ Don't trust everything to memory. Make a list. Keep just one list going at a time. It will free your mind for more important things, such as a chess game or daydreaming. To-do lists are not simply reminders; they're reinforcement. It's harder to procrastinate when something is written down.

▲ Each week (Sunday evening is a good time), list phone calls to make, errands to do, projects to finish, and other activities that must be done by the end of the week. Note each activity, such as "call the dentist" or "buy a new suit for the convention this weekend." To the left of the activity, put the day of the week and approximately how much time it might take. For example, "Fri., 45 min." Then add it to your planner for that day.

▲ Each evening, look at your planner for the next day (evenings are better than mornings, in case you have an early meeting to prepare for). Add to your list things you need to do tomorrow, including what you didn't get done today. If you're going to the post office, make a note to take your packages; if you're going to the supermarket, make a note to take bottles and sacks for recycling.

▲ Always make your list on the same size and type of paper. Don't use the back of an envelope or receipt. It might get thrown away. Put your list in a prominent place, the same place every day.

▲ When an item is completed, check it or cross it off. Make sure the letter is mailed or the laundry is picked up before you check it off. If you didn't get something done, schedule it for the next available day. After transferring the "undones" to your next list, throw away the old to-do list. Deal with each item in some way, even if it is to decide not to do it.

If you have trouble locating your list, try this: Buy a pad of lined paper in a color that you want to be your "list color." You may want to design your own sheet or use the following sample and copy it onto your list-color paper of choice. It should be noticeable and a color that you don't use for any other writing—like goldenrod, cherry pink, or sky blue with clouds. Buy the size that fits into your planner without sticking out around the edges. Also purchase sticky notes of the same color. Keep a pad by your bed, in the car, attached to the refrigerator with a magnet, in the bathroom, in your purse, on your desk at work, or any other place where you would be apt to have a bright idea. Then, anytime you think of something, you can write it down right then and there. As soon as possible, stick the note on your current list, or in your planner if it's something to do at a later date.

Your list might look something like this:

Sample To-Do List

Day _____

Phone Calls

Name	Number	Subject
Pearl	444-1234	Party invitations
Dr. Molar	666-4321	Dentist appointment

Projects/Activities

Wash clothes

Write letters

Appointments

When	What/Whom	Where
2:45 p.m.	Haircut—Jan	50th and Dodge

Errands

Where	What to Take
Library	Overdue books
Recycling site	Newspapers and aluminum cans

Be a Time-Saver

If you have lots to do and little time to do it, these tips are for you:

▲ **Know why you procrastinate.** Identify what you put off and why: can be done by someone else (why not delegate?), too difficult (could you get some help?), not fun (have a friend do it with you?), or not really important (why do it?). If you have an unpleasant task, give yourself a deadline and plan a great reward for yourself when you finish.

▲ **Do it right the first time!** "If you don't have time to do it right, when will you have time to do it over?"[7]

▲ **Set aside certain times of the day to do nothing but make and take phone calls.** The numbers should already be on your list. (Looking up all the numbers at once saves time.) When the phone rings at times other than your designated "phone time"—and if your callers don't need to talk with you immediately or if the calls aren't relevant at the moment, arrange to call back and note the "phone appointment" in your planner. Alternatively, let your answering machine take over and screen your calls. When you do accept calls, keep them brief by setting a timer or by standing while you're on the phone.

▲ **Use self-discipline.** Remind yourself of the importance of getting things done. Concentrate on what you're doing. Focus on one project at a time, anticipate distractions and avoid them, do the toughest tasks first if possible, and find the location most conducive to your work.

▲ **Follow through until you're finished.** If you jump from job to job, you may waste time and lose momentum reminding yourself where you stopped, where your supplies are, or what your goal was.

▲ **When you check your Monthly Agenda, look to see what cards and gifts you need to buy.** Buy them all at once.

▲ **Take inventory of your supply needs and stock up weekly or at least monthly:** stamps, envelopes, greeting cards, staples, batteries. This will save you many hours and many unnecessary trips to the store. (Check chapter 7 for a list of office supplies to have on hand.)

▲ **Make up a gift wrapping/mailing kit and keep it handy.** Include wrapping paper, ribbons, gift cards, scotch tape, scissors, boxes, and labels. You might hide the kit under the bed if others are inclined to borrow some of the items.

▲ **Delegate responsibility to other members of your family.**

▲ **Just say "no" to requests that you don't have time to honor or that aren't really in tune with your priorities.**

▲ **Use the phone or Internet first when you're not sure where to go for certain products and services.**

▲ **Set out a special basket or bowl for everyone to put their keys in.** Have at least four sets of keys. Hide three sets.

General Time-Management Techniques and Tools

In business and at home, use planning systems to make things run more smoothly and give you some control.

▲ **Plan ahead.** Anticipate pitfalls and time-wasters before you begin a large project. Divide it into many small projects so it's not overwhelming. If you're fixing a huge dinner, decide what you can do a week ahead of time, the day before, and so on. Estimate how much time you'll need and when to schedule tasks; consider potential delays. Then set deadlines. Have small goals: daily, weekly, and final. Line up human and material resources ahead of time. Evaluate the process as you go along.

▲ **As suggested earlier, plan backwards.** Decide when you need to have everything done for your huge dinner—say, two hours ahead of time. Make deadlines for buying items like candles, napkins, or new glasses; for making freezable items; and for sending invitations. List all steps and whether the project spans a period of days, weeks, or months. Write each step and deadline in your planner. You should also have a list of all steps in a folder you create for this specific project.

▲ **Know your prime time or high-productivity times as well as your low-productivity times.** If you're sharp and alert at midnight, that's the time to balance your checkbook or compute your income tax. Do easy tasks that require less thought or concentration during your low-productivity times.

▲ **Respect your planner and lists.** Make them realistic and flexible.

▲ **Make time for yourself.** You can't accomplish anything unless you schedule time to recharge your batteries in the way that works best for you.

Holidays: Are They Really Happy?

Do you get caught up in the trappings (or the traps) of the holiday season and tend to overbuy, overspend, overcommit, overbake, overeat, and generally overdo? Instead of feeling peaceful, hopeful, and reverent during these sacred days, do you feel rushed, frustrated, and stressed? When you're in the midst of this "overness," you need to remind yourself that even if you win the rat race, you're still a rat (a figure of speech, of course). So, how can you avoid the rat race?

First, begin by consulting the wisdom of your heart as well as your mind. Is your goal to enjoy meaningful fellowship with friends and a peaceful time with your family, or to impress the neighbors or live up to your great-aunt's expectations?

Your second challenge is to plan. When planning, be aware of the consequences of your choices during the holiday season. Picture the week after! Do you see yourself standing in long gift-exchange lines? Mortgaging your home? Coping with a seasonal cold?

Planning will lead to better choices. Here are seven tips:

▲ **Simplify.** If you typically entertain, shop, send cards, bake, decorate, wrap, and attend numerous gatherings, drop one or two activities, or do part of some.

▲ **Share the joy.** Let your family members participate...meaningfully.

▲ **Pre-plan.** If you plan a lot of activities, use a big sheet of paper to plan before filling in your regular planner.

▲ **Family plan.** Fill in your planner with your family plan for the season.

▲ **Think ahead.** Keep a running gift list throughout the year.

▲ **Use the Internet to shop.** You can compare prices and view your selections. Most online stores will wrap, include gift cards, and mail. All you have to do is pay!

▲ **Give the gift of organizing to a friend or family member.** Visit the National Association of Professional Organizers Web site at www.NAPO.net to find a professional organizer in your area.

Checklist: What You Learned

This chapter showed you how to do the following:

❏ Find the perfect planner for your needs.
❏ Choose types of items to put in your planner.
❏ List and prioritize errands.
❏ Make it a habit to check your planner daily.
❏ Master at least three time-savers.

Some later chapters address time-saving activities such as

▲ Setting up an efficient home office with the proper equipment (chapter 7).

▲ Getting rid of clutter—it causes confusion (chapter 4).

▲ Creating a good family communication center (chapter 7).

Using the time-management techniques in chapters 1, 2, and 3, you can now make time for organizing your home (or belongings).

Part II

Simply Organize...
Your Stuff

Your Storage: Where Do Your Belongings Belong?

This chapter is a step-by-step plan for sorting out your things. Read the entire chapter to see what's involved before you start. This is not simply a closet-by-closet cleanup, but instead a comprehensive plan for putting your belongings in order.

Specifically, you'll learn how to do the following:

▲ Create a master plan for all your belongings by rethinking your current storage patterns

▲ Find or create convenient, efficient, and attractive places for everything you store or use

When determining storage, consider flexibility, availability, neatness, and convenience. There are no hard-and-fast rules. You may have to redo and rethink some of your storage ideas as you go along. You may want to tackle this project with a friend who will offer suggestions, give you ideas, and make it more fun.

Before you write anything, take a long and thoughtful walk through your home. Open every door, cupboard, and drawer. See what you have and where there is potential for storage. While you are walking (and thinking), consider how you can do things differently. Ask yourself where the most convenient areas are; ask yourself what items you use the most; then ask yourself to sit down and take a break from all that walking and thinking.

As you contemplate what you have and where to put it, remember that there are no set ways to store things. Everyone's needs are different. Do what works best for your household.

Inventory Valuables and Diagram Your Space

For insurance claims and other purposes, it's a good idea to have a list plus photos or a video of your important belongings. During your household tour, make notes about these items as you come across them. Enter them into an inventory along with their values for insurance purposes and for your heirs. Keep a copy of the inventory with your insurance papers and your will.

It's also useful to make a diagram of your home and then "name and claim" rooms: Determine what should be stored in the room or nearby and indicate the main function of each room. Off-the-shelf and online software is available for both inventorying and diagramming your home; or you can use your built-in spreadsheet (such as Excel or Lotus 1-2-3) for the inventory.

But First, a Test

This little exam is designed to show you how much time you waste when your belongings are not where they belong.

To see how much time you can save when you organize your home, estimate the amount of time it would take you to

1. Find the spare key for the back door.
2. Obtain your official birth certificate.
3. Locate photos of your honeymoon (or another memorable trip).
4. Find a new roll of film (without going to a store).
5. Gift-wrap a package.
6. Prepare a package for mailing.
7. Find an extension cord, a pair of scissors, or two AAA batteries.

Bonus Questions

8. How many seconds would it take you to locate your emergency first-aid chart?

9. How many junk drawers do you have?

10. How many junk drawers do you want to have?

Before you begin, consider your clutter. Barbara Hemphill, author of *Taming the Paper Tiger,* says that clutter is postponed decisions. What is your clutter?

It's important to know what your clutter consists of; one person's clutter may be another's insurance policy. Henry David Thoreau wrote, "Have nothing in your house that you do not know to be useful or believe to be beautiful." He probably had no clutter…or junk mail.

Basically, clutter is something that is in the wrong place at the wrong time. If my best silver tray is sticking out from under the couch, it's clutter; if it's sitting under a German chocolate cake, it's a treasure. Here are five reasons to conquer clutter:

▲ To be able to find what you really need before it grows bacteria and while you still remember why you need it.

▲ To have more time for things that really matter, such as exercising, gardening, spending time with your children, or writing the Great American Novel.

▲ To have more money. Practice "preventive clutter management"–buy less–and save money. Have a garage sale and *make* money. Give items to charity and take an income-tax deduction.

▲ To create a workspace for cooking, working on your income tax forms, or assembling your model airplane.

▲ To have less to clean, dust, repair, sort, alphabetize, or conceal from company.

Only you know what clutters your life. When a possession has a meaning and a place of its own, it becomes something of value.

Seven Steps to Organizing Your Possessions

The following sections show you the steps to follow to organize your stuff.

Step 1: List Categories of Your Possessions

First, list the types of possessions you have that require storage (that is, almost everything). Use the following list of suggested categories and add your own:

Your Possessions

_____ Clothing (see chapter 5); list by person or category

_____ Memorabilia, photos, letters (see chapter 6)

_____ Mail, miscellaneous papers (see chapter 6)

_____ Financial papers (see chapter 6)

_____ Games

_____ Books

_____ Magazines

_____ Outdoor tools, machines

_____ Holiday, seasonal decorations

_____ Blankets, bed linens

_____ Luggage (including shaving kits, hanging protectors, and cosmetic cases)

_____ Paint, paint supplies

_____ Toys; listed by child or age group

_____ Kitchen items

_____ Picnic supplies

_____ Sewing items

_____ Camera equipment, film, and batteries

_____ Cosmetics

_____ Medicines

_____ Bar items

_____ Silverware

_____ Silver serving and display items

_____ China

_____ Sports equipment

_____ Crafts

_____ Cleaning supplies

_____ Projects

_____ Club/civic organization work

_____ Gift-wrapping supplies

_____ Camping gear

_____ Hobbies

_____ Decorating items

_____ Plant-care items

_____ Unused furniture

_____ _____

_____ _____

_____ _____

_____ _____

_____ _____

_____ _____

_____ _____

Next, make an Item Category List that looks like this:

Item Category List

1. Item Category	2. Current Storage	3. New Storage

In this step, you'll fill in only column 1. List the types of possessions you have that require storage (that is, almost everything).

The following are some suggestions. Depending on your family's activities and interests, you might have several categories, such as books, clothing, tools, and games. When you have different "owners" in your household for the same types of items, show the individual's names. Leave plenty of room in column 1 for changes and additions—better use a pencil!

Sample Item Category List

1. Item Category	2. Current Storage	3. New Storage
Financial papers	_____	_____
Photos	_____	_____
Luggage	_____	_____
Books	_____	_____
Reference (Jim)	_____	_____
Old–first editions	_____	_____
Professional	_____	_____
Text books (Robin)	_____	_____
Children's (Ellie)	_____	_____

Step 2: List Where Your Belongings Are Currently Stored

Now fill in column 2 of your Item Category List. Find where your belongings are now stored and write the location or locations next to the items. For "floating" items—those kept nowhere in particular—write "none" in column 2. Such homeless items might include the mail (if your family members play hide-and-seek to find their letters) or your out-of-season clothes. If your bikini is stuffed in a drawer next to your ski sweaters, this would be a good time to find a home for both of them.

Step 3: List Your Potential Storage Areas

Now make a separate Storage List. Use the form at the end of this section to write on or use as a guide. Designate whether the areas or containers are large (A), medium (B), or smaller than a breadbox (C). Here are some examples of the different sizes:

A. **Large:** Outdoor shed, good-sized closet, areas in the attic or basement, any room or part of a room used exclusively for storage....

B. **Medium:** Trunk, chest, dresser, cabinet, cupboard, shelving, file cabinet, small closet....

C. **Smaller than a breadbox:** Baskets, photo boxes, small drawers, toolkits, small crates, containers you can carry....

Work from top to bottom and from east to west (or north to south...what matters is that you progress in the same direction to avoid duplicating your efforts or backtracking). You might start, for example, with the attic closet and end with the basement, garage, and then the shed.

List every potential storage area and container, including those for clothing, papers, and office items (which are all discussed in detail in later chapters).

One family's Storage List might begin something like this:

Example Storage List

Storage	Size
Attic	
Large closet	(A)
Cedar closet	(A)
Blue trunk	(B)
Storage boxes	(C)
Guest bedroom	
Closet	(A)
Dresser #1	(B)
Dresser #2	(B)
Telephone stand	(C)
Shelf above bed	(C)
John's bedroom	
Walk-in closet	(A)
File cabinet	(B)
Pegboard	(B)
Small wicker chest	(C)
Toolbox	(C)
Guest bathroom	
Medicine chest	(B)
Hamper	(B)
Cosmetic case	(C)
Mary's bedroom	
Closet	(A)
Dressing table	(B)
Bulletin board	(C)
Sewing basket	(C)

Storage List

List your available storage, room by room, and the size (A, B, or C, as described on page 80). Don't try to decide right now what to store in each area and container. That comes later.

Storage	Size

Step 4: Rethink and Reorganize Your Storage

When considering where to put what, use the Item Category List you made in step 1. You now have three types of decisions to make: what to personalize, what to consolidate, and what to divide up.

Things to Personalize

Many items considered *personal* are best classified by their owner. Family members undoubtedly have their own clothes and possibly books, games, sports equipment, bedroom furniture, toys, cosmetics, medicines, hobby supplies, and other items as well. You'll probably want to keep some of these in each person's bedroom (for example, clothes, games, compact discs, and some books), or classify them as bathroom items (such as cosmetics and medicines). Write a *P* next to the personal items you want to store individually.

Things to Consolidate

You may want to consolidate some personal items with those of other family members (shared hobby supplies, luggage, some books, and sports equipment, for example). Indicate with a *C* the items you want to store together or consolidate.

You might also want to consolidate many common items—those that don't belong to individual family members.

You won't know what you have until you put it all together. You may have holiday decorations that would fill a shopping mall and enough picnic supplies for the Woodstock reunion.

Things to Separate

As important as it is to consolidate some types of items, it's just as important to separate others–winter and summer clothing for example, or financial papers from appliance warranties and everyday silverware from heirloom silver. You might want to divide broad categories into smaller separate ones, in fact, and indicate the change on your Item Category List. For example:

Column 1
Sports equipment
Golf
Baseball
Fishing

Step 5: Assign New Storage

On your Storage List, you're almost ready to assign items, or types of items, to storage receptacles. Use a pencil; you may change your mind often. First, though, consider the following:

▲ Before making any major changes, consult all family members. They may have some valuable ideas. They need to be involved in the process so they will understand, appreciate, and contribute to your storage system–and so they'll know where to find things later!

▲ You'll need a well-lit room for your home office and a communication center that's convenient for all family members.

▲ Allow plenty of extra room when planning your list so you can add things later.

▲ Put things where they are the most convenient. If the storage isn't useful, it won't be used. Items used for hobbies, meal preparation, studying, decorating, sports, cleaning, carpentry, and other activities should be as close as possible to where they're used.

▲ Make sure things are reachable. An item might be in the right room or closet, but if your arms can't reach it, it might as well be in the attic. The more something is used, the easier it should be to get. Store things you never want to see again, but must save, in those hard-to-reach places. Items you use often should be accessible!

▲ For each item or category, consider how often, where, and when you use it (summer, Christmas, Passover); who uses it most; how much space it needs; and what related items you might want to store with it.

▲ Identify items that aren't worth the trouble of storing and make a note to sell, donate, or discard them.

▲ Be aware of particular items' environmental requirements; can they tolerate direct sun or cold, hot, dry, or damp conditions? You probably wouldn't, for example, put your classic vinyl record collection next to a south window or over a floor register…or your wedding dress in a damp basement.

▲ Designate or create a special place for "errand items"—to be returned to a store, a friend, school, or the library; as well as film to be developed, shoes to replace, dry cleaning to drop off, and parcels to mail. This special place should be near the door you use most often when going on errands. I suggest special shelves, a box, or a dresser.

One more thing before you start assigning new storage: It would be wise to scan the suggestions in the remainder of this chapter, if you haven't already done so, for the bathroom and kitchen, children's items, and miscellaneous items.

Now you're ready to complete column 3 of your Item Category List ("New Storage"), referring to your Storage List for available space.

▲ Use a pencil; you'll probably change your mind as you go.

▲ Skip clothing, papers, and office items for now. We'll deal with them in later chapters.

Step 6: Make Plans to Move Your Stuff!

There are a few things you can do to get yourself in the right frame of mind for moving your items to their new storage places:

▲ Gather large boxes and trash bags.

▲ Find an honest friend with good taste to help you make judgement calls.

▲ Mark in your planner with big red letters, "Storage Moving Day."

▲ Tell everyone you are leaving the country.

▲ Take your phone off the hook.

▲ Have your meals delivered.

▲ Call your favorite charity to come next week, and,

▲ Dig in!

Get the Kids Involved in a Garage Sale

Reorganizing your storage creates a good opportunity for your children to weed out their things, have a garage sale, and keep the proceeds. They have fun and their rooms get cleaned. But keep track of what they're selling; you might lose some silverware or valuable antiques if they get carried away!

Step 7: Dig In!

First, decide where to begin. For purposes of illustration, we'll say you're starting with an attic closet. Remove everything, with the possible exception of extremely heavy or cumbersome items that will remain there anyway. Even if you don't move the big stuff, look under and around it; you might find treasures, broken buttons, or gum wrappers.

Gather all the items that you'll store in the attic closet and place them nearby. If you want to make a game of it, have a family scavenger hunt in which family members hunt down and relocate items you designate—holiday items to the attic closet, sporting equipment to the back hallway, games to the den, and so on.

Now you have an empty attic closet and you've gathered things to put into it. Clean (vacuum and dust or wash) the area and plan the arrangement before filling it. Decide which items to put in first and where each item will go.

Put smaller articles in see-through or clearly labeled containers. Place boxes of ornaments, wrapping supplies, or holiday cards in front of larger items (the tree stand, the artificial tree, or the life-size stuffed Rudolph). It's usually best to locate all the like items together (except for items that would be affected by the extreme hot and cold temperatures of the attic). If you store Christmas plates in the dining room cabinet, will you remember them next year?

Here are some suggestions for general storage:

▲ Leave aisles in large storage areas if possible. Unless everything is easily accessible and in plain sight, storage will be less useful, the area may not remain orderly, and items will be hard to find.

▲ Allow extra room. You may have more luggage than you realize, or you may want to add to your collection. Most people bring more items into the home every day than they take out!

▲ When possible, keep things off the floor, where they're more likely to become lost, wet, or damaged. Even file cabinets and large containers should be on boards or bricks in attic, basement, garage, and outdoor storage areas. For some articles, you may want to use pegboard, hooks, open shelves, or bookcases.

▲ As mentioned earlier, it's sometimes necessary to divide a category into smaller units. For instance, if you have hundreds of books to store, dividing them into subjects—fiction, science, history, "how-to" books, humor, and so on—makes them easier to locate. You might even get ambitious and label the shelves so others will be able to find books easily and replace them properly.

▲ Make sure you label all the boxes clearly. Otherwise, your family won't know—and even you might not remember—that the Christmas tree is in the baby-crib box. You also may want to create a rough map of what's stored where so you'll remember to look in the back-left corner of the attic for the hockey equipment.

Storage Ideas

(For clothing, see chapter 5; for paper and office items, see chapters 6 and 7.)

▲ Wrapping packages is convenient if you use a large under-bed storage box to hold everything you need: gift wrap and bags, tissue paper, ribbon, bows, scissors, tape for wrapping gifts and sealing parcels, address labels, enclosure cards, pens, padded mailing envelopes—whatever you use regularly.

▲ Store bed linens in an under-bed storage box.

▲ Large baskets with hinged lids can do double duty as coffee tables and game storage.

▲ Trunks and footlockers are good for storing linens, children's schoolwork, and some types of collections.

▲ Shallow storage can be built into walls, just as medicine cabinets are, for ironing centers, spice cabinets, or small pantries.

▲ Use drawer dividers everywhere you want to keep unlike items separated and multiple items tidy. Putting away and retrieving things is a snap.

▲ Place a small basket or box on a shelf near where games are played. Whenever you find a stray game piece or playing card, put it in the basket or box. Later you can return it to its proper place, or find it there when you get out that puzzle or game again.

▲ Use a tackle box for sewing items.

▲ Plastic see-through containers are ideal for everything from clothes to photos.

▲ Have only one junk drawer...but have one.

Toys and Other Children's Items

▲ Many specialty stores carry items such as colorful children's lockers, towel ladders, and laundry carts–great for storing children's toys.

▲ Mount shallow magazine racks on the insides of closet doors to hold children's books, tapes, or CDs.

▲ It's easier for kids to hang clothes and towels on hooks than to put them on hangers and racks. Hooks are useful on closet doors, bathroom walls, and kitchen cupboards. Hall trees are great in bedrooms, large bathrooms, and, of course, halls.

▲ Pegboard, once available only in brown but now sold in dozens of colors, is attractive and versatile in many rooms and storage areas.

▲ Tiered wire baskets can hold small toys and game pieces.

Kitchen Storage Tips

▲ Take anything out of your kitchen cupboards that isn't used for cooking, serving, or eating. Put things like picnic items, flower vases, and camping cookware in other areas, such as the basement or more remote storage areas. This way, you'll be able to avoid stacking unmatched plates and nesting five casserole dishes.

▲ Shelf paper is usually unnecessary. If you insist on it, however, use adhesive-backed paper and remove only the outside inch of the backing. This way, you'll have a smooth surface and a little more cushion. The shelf paper is also easy to remove when you're tired of it.

▲ You can also use washable wallpaper for lining shelves.

▲ Place clear plastic runners under the sink or in areas where spills are likely to happen. The runners are easy to cut and easy to wash. They also look good.

▲ Hang hooks in various spots in your kitchen–in the cupboard for cups, inside a closet door for towels, or inside a cupboard door for utensils.

▲ Use pegboard on a wall or in the back of a cupboard or closet to hang almost anything.

▲ Recycling bins can be stacked to save space.

▲ Inside cabinet doors, post information such as measure equivalents, favorite recipes, and first-aid procedures.

▲ Don't overfill drawers with utensils such as cheese shredders and potato peelers. You should be able to see what you have without moving anything.

▲ Keep refrigerator storage containers, wrap, and bags near the sink if that is where you fill them with leftovers.

▲ Have your children clip coupons for food and other groceries and give them the money you save.

▲ Store extra appliances and dishes in the basement or storeroom.

Food: Storage and Shopping

▲ Ask the butcher to package meat in individual serving sizes.

▲ Use glass or clear-plastic containers for storing food in your refrigerator so you always know what you are saving...and you can see how green it gets.

▲ To save time, know your grocery store intimately and make a master list of what is stocked where. Make out your grocery list in the order in which items are arranged in the store.

▲ Put a long cord on the kitchen phone—or get a cordless one—so you can cook or clean while talking.

Bathroom Storage Ideas

▲ To add storage in your bathroom, get a ladder towel rack (which holds lots of towels) or sink a cabinet into the wall.

▲ If possible, hang washcloths, towels, and robes on hooks—hooks are easier to use (thus more likely to be used) than racks.

▲ Color-coordinate towels and washcloths, assigning a different color to each family member. That way, everyone will know who leaves theirs in a pile on the floor and how many they have out at one time.

▲ Put hand towels in a small wicker basket or a wooden wine rack. They are handy and decorative.

Other Products for Organizing Your Goods and Treasures

▲ *Storage for collections: shadow boxes, glass-front cabinets*

▲ *Simple hand-held labelers to create attractive labels for your storage shelves and cabinets*

▲ *Carts on wheels with wire baskets for office supplies, hobby supplies, and toys*

▲ *Carts on wheels with racks for hanging files for a portable office*

Following are some of the catalog sources for organizing products:

▲ *Lillian Vernon: 1-800-545-5426; www.lillianvernon.com*

▲ *Hold Everything: 1-800-421-2285*

▲ *Get Organized: 1-800-803-9400; www.getorginc.com*

▲ *Exposures: 1-800-572-5750; www.exposuresonline.com*

Checklist: What You Learned

This chapter showed you how to do the following things:

- ❏ List and inventory possessions.
- ❏ List current storage of belongings.
- ❏ List potential storage and designate size: large (A), medium (B), or small (C).
- ❏ Develop a new master storage plan.
- ❏ Assign new storage.
- ❏ Buy or find storage containers.
- ❏ Move items into new storage areas.

By now you have developed storage methods. You've walked through your home, analyzed your storage needs, and identified potential storage areas. You have an idea of what to consolidate and separate. Soon everything will be stored neatly and conveniently, each item in a designated place. Your plan is flexible–you can always change, add, subtract, or throw away.

Now let's move on to chapter 5, where you'll learn to store and care for your clothing.

Clothes, Clothes Everywhere...and Not a Thing to Wear

How would you like to find some new outfits...have closets roomy enough that your clothes don't wrinkle...get dressed in half the time it normally takes you? Sound good? Then adopt these goals!

▲ To have all closets, drawers, and other clothing storage areas so clean and organized that you can and probably will wear anything in them.

▲ To catch up on all mending, cleaning, and repairing of clothing and accessories.

▲ To develop and use systems for staying on top of these tasks.

Chances are, if you listed every article of clothing in your home, you would be overwhelmed, not to mention overtired. We tend to hang on to an article of unwearable clothing for a variety of reasons:

▲ It may come back in style (has it ever?).

▲ "I may lose (or gain) 15 pounds."

▲ "My favorite aunt gave it to me."

▲ "I may need it someday...for something...."

▲ It would make a good paint shirt (but you already have eight paint shirts and you don't even paint).

On a regular basis, you probably wear no more than 30 percent of what is hanging in your closet; but you look through 100 percent of it when you're deciding what to wear. You'll never wear many of these items. But maybe you would if

▲ ...you could find the matching belt.

▲ ...it were hemmed.

▲ ...the buttons were all there.

▲ ...you could find a shirt to go with it.

▲ ...it weren't stained.

Make up your mind to tackle these problems and add 5...10...even a dozen or more items to your wardrobe at little or no expense.

Before you begin, do the following:

▲ Arm yourself with large trash bags, small drawstring trash-can liners, large boxes, a permanent marker, some tags, and some yarn.

▲ Dedicate your week to sorting, tossing, giving away, washing, mending, and properly storing your clothing items and accessories.

Step 1: Scout Out Clothing and Storage for It

Survey your storage situation; walk around your home and look in every conceivable place an article of clothing or an accessory could be hiding.

As you survey the situation, tape-record your ideas or carry a clipboard and take notes, keeping the following questions in mind:

▲ What are each person's clothing needs and current storage situation?

▲ How many family members need clothing-storage areas?

▲ What kinds of closets and drawers would best accommodate them?

▲ Should I store each individual's clothing items separately? Should there be shared storage areas for items such as seasonal and athletic clothing?

Step 2: Decide What to Put Where

When you've decided what should go where, note your choices on the Clothing Worksheet. For example,

1. Out of season: cedar closet in attic

2. Hand-me-downs: guest-room closet

3. Current season's coats, jackets, and accessories: front-hall closet

4. Special athletic clothing: back-hallway closet

5. Memorabilia, such as letter sweaters and poodle skirts (costume potential): guest-room closet

6. Rarely worn clothing, such as ball gowns: cedar closet in attic

You can add your own categories at the end of the Clothing Worksheet.

Clothing Worksheet	
Type of Clothing or Accessory	**Storage Area or Container**
1. Out of season	_____ _____ _____ _____
2. Hand-me-downs	_____ _____ _____ _____
3. Current season's outdoor wear	_____ _____ _____ _____

(continues)

(continued)

Type of Clothing or Accessory	Storage Area or Container
4. Special athletic clothing	
5. Memorabilia	
6. Rarely worn items	
7. My clothing	
8. Spouse's clothing	
9. Maternity/baby clothes	

Type of Clothing or Accessory	Storage Area or Container
10. Heirlooms, wedding dress	
11. Paint smocks, aprons, work clothes	
12. Other	
13. Other	
14. Other	
15. Other	

Step 3: Design Your Storage Areas

In step 2, you determined where to store specific items. Now, go back to the Clothing Worksheet and write how you want to arrange things and what you need to buy. For example:

▲ Storage of seasonal clothing and formal wear: cedar closet in attic

Will need two trunks for sweaters, shelf for plastic bags of scarves and mittens, padded hangers and clear garment bags for formals. Will put trunks on west wall, hang garment bags on right side, and hang winter coats and jackets on left side.

▲ Storage of athletic clothing and equipment: back-hallway closet

Will need large mug rack to hang swimsuits and coverups, pegboard for ski goggles and gloves, an old bookshelf for football shoes and walking shoes.

▲ Storage of office, leisure, and evening wear, including accessories and shoes: my bedroom

Will need large dresser for undergarments, pajamas, tee shirts; shelves in closet for shoes; plastic crate in closet for old work shoes and sandals; four adhesive cork squares to hang jewelry on closet wall; clear plastic shoe bag to hold hose and scarves; open plastic shower-curtain hooks for hanging belts; wicker trunk for sweaters; under-bed storage boxes for summer clothes.

Tips for Storing Jewelry

▲ Mount cork-board squares on a door or wall—in a closet or above a dresser, for example. Hang necklaces, bracelets, rings, and other jewelry from pushpins (the kind with large plastic heads) stuck into the cork.

▲ Use a tackle box for storing larger costume jewelry such as bracelets, beads, and large earrings.

▲ Put silverware containers in your bedroom drawers for costume jewelry.

▲ Expandable mug racks and clear plastic shoeboxes also work well for large jewelry.

▲ A compartmentalized cosmetics case is useful for storing jewelry.

Tips for Hanging Clothes

▲ Check out specialty stores that have a varied selection of storage items, such as colorful children's lockers.

▲ As mentioned earlier, it's easier to hang clothes on hooks than on hangers and racks. Installing hooks on closet doors, on bathroom walls, and in kitchen cupboards—and setting out hall trees in bedrooms and other strategic locations—will keep things off the floor. Your clothes will look better, last longer, and require less laundering.

▲ Sturdy mug racks or closet hooks are good for clothes you've worn but aren't yet ready to launder, and for jogging clothes that need to dry out before going into the laundry basket.

Tips for Storing Hosiery and Other Small Accessories

▲ To hang scarves, use clothespins or clips on wire hangers.

▲ Attach large plastic clips to wall- or door-mounted cork squares. The clips will secure scarves, fabric belts, and headbands without cutting into the fabric.

▲ Use stackable plastic boxes or tiered wire racks or baskets for shoes, scarves, jewelry, socks, gloves, belts, hose, purses, and hats.

▲ Clear-plastic hanging shoe bags on the insides of closet doors can hold pantyhose, scarves, shoulder pads, small purses, fabric belts, jewelry, socks, and more. In a coat closet, they can hold scarves, mittens, and gloves.

▲ Expanding mug racks can be useful in your clothes closet for storing scarves, belts, necklaces, ties, or fabric purses.

▲ Put a small dresser or a plastic storage unit with drawers under short hanging clothes (blouses, jackets, skirts) in your closet. You can use the dresser for scarves, purses, belts, and socks. Make sure the drawers have *clear* plastic fronts so that you can easily see what's in them.

▲ Save time and spare yourself some aggravation: Whenever possible, use clear-plastic garment bags, sweater bags, and boxes.

▲ A basket near the front (or back) door can hold mittens and scarves.

▲ Hang wicker bicycle baskets on the wall—one for each family member's mittens, gloves, and scarves.

▲ Under-bed storage boxes can hold sweaters, sweatshirts, out-of-season clothing, and good purses.

▲ Hang belts from plastic shower hooks (the ones that don't snap shut) in your closet, one or two belts on each hook. You can hang the hooks from the rod side by side or vertically in chainlike fashion, depending on how much room you have.

▲ Don't put away unmatched socks and stockings. You'll avoid the frustration of pulling out socks with no mates, or of being unable to find the odd sock once you've located its partner. Better yet, as you're folding the laundry, roll each pair of matching socks together into a ball by turning under the cuffs. Store them in a clear plastic box in your sock drawer or a mesh bag in your closet.

▲ Store shoes on a closet shelf or on a bookcase in the closet. They'll be off the floor, and thus cleaner and easier to reach.

▲ Specialty shops have towel ladders, laundry carts on wheels, and many other containers that are great for clothing storage.

▲ Put shallow boxes of different sizes in drawers to contain lots of little things (such as curlers, cosmetics, and ponytail holders) and smallish things (socks and undergarments).

Step 4: Collect Containers for Clothing Storage

Here are some suggestions for your clothing-storage shopping list. You probably have additional ideas of your own.

▲ Plastic or wicker baskets

▲ Tiered wire baskets

▲ Bicycle baskets

▲ Corkboard squares

▲ Pushpins

▲ Clear-plastic hanging shoe bags

▲ Clear-plastic shoeboxes

▲ Mesh bags

▲ Cabinets, dressers

▲ Under-bed storage boxes

▲ Clear-plastic garment bags

▲ Colorful children's lockers

▲ Hall tree

▲ Rolling laundry cart

▲ Padded hangers

▲ Trunks

▲ Open shower-curtain hooks

▲ Plastic or wooden mug racks

▲ Pegboard and pegboard attachments

▲ Plastic crates

Step 5: Sort One Closet at a Time

Now that you have your plan written down, concentrate on one person's clothing at a time. Start with your own closets, drawers, baskets, trunks, dressers, cabinets, or hooks. Start with one area, such as your main closet. Remove everything. Yes, everything!!! Even empty hangers. When you get items out of the closet, they somehow look different and it's easier to make decisions about them.

Got closet anxiety? If you're not sure you can handle taking everything out of the closet at one time, start with items that don't belong because they

- ▲ Are not apparel items
- ▲ Need mending
- ▲ Are incomplete outfits (you have nothing to wear with them)
- ▲ Require cleaning or ironing
- ▲ Are of sentimental value only
- ▲ Belong to someone else
- ▲ Are out of style or "out of size"

Put these items in separate piles—one for ironing; one for mending; others for stuff to be given away, returned to the owner, and so forth. Then put the piles where they belong (in the sewing room, the laundry room, and the car, for example).

Now you can take out the rest of the clothes and deal with them. Look at all the room you have!

Get Rid of Stuff!

Go through everything you've removed from storage and decide what to get rid of. Surely you can persuade yourself to part with

- ▲ Items that have irreparable tears or permanent stains
- ▲ Things that don't look good on you or that aren't your color
- ▲ Out-of-style clothes...they never come back quite the same way

Next, determine how to dispose of the unwanted items. Depending on their condition, you might

▲ Donate them to the Salvation Army, Goodwill, AMVETS, or other charitable organization.

▲ Take them to a consignment shop.

▲ Give them to relatives or friends.

▲ Put them in the trash.

▲ Sell them at a garage sale.

Until you actually deliver the items to the Salvation Army or have your garage sale, put them in a designated box, bag, or basket located where it won't be overlooked. Also, label it clearly so that the contents aren't mistaken for trash.

Relocate Items

As I suggested previously, relocate every item that needs mending, washing, dry cleaning, or accessorizing. Here are a few suggestions:

▲ Put it in a pile for the dry cleaner.

▲ Put it in the laundry pile or in a large plastic bag for ironing.

▲ Put it in the mending pile or sewing basket.

▲ Put it in the "need-to-buy-something-to-wear-with-it" pile.

▲ Put it in the pile to go to another closet (attic cedar closet, guest room, another bedroom).

▲ Put it in the "undecided" pile.

▲ Put it in the pile to go back into the closet.

In other words, nothing should go back into the closet if it isn't currently wearable—and that means "in season" as well as "in style" and "in good repair." Look through your other closets and drawers to determine whether there is anything in those that should be stored in the closet you're now working on.

Refill the Closet and Attack the Piles

While the closet is empty, clean it. Wipe down the shelves; sweep, vacuum, or wash the floor; and dust the rods. Before putting anything back in the closet, scrutinize each article, one at a time.

When you do put things back, arrange them by function—professional, formal, leisure, work, and athletic, for example. Make sure that everything you wear on a regular basis is visible, so that when you get dressed you'll be able to find what you want to wear and retrieve it quickly.

Next, attack the "need-to-buy-something-to-wear-with-it pile. Make a list of articles of clothing and accessories you need to complete an outfit or fill out your wardrobe. You might wear that blue dress if you had a scarf to match. A pair of taupe shoes could complete three outfits you currently avoid.

Now follow the same procedure with all your other clothing-storage areas: other closets, baskets, trunks, dressers, hooks, and cabinets. When you've completed your personal clothing areas, move on to the next challenge. Keep moving until you have dealt with the entire household's clothing (with help and consultation from each person whose wardrobe is being culled and rearranged). You'll discover that you have much more room in your storage areas and that you all have "new" outfits to wear as a result of your reorganization.

Step 6: Wrap It Up and Move It Out!

When you've cleaned out all your clothing areas and organized everyone's clothing and accessories, you need to deal with the by-products: the trash bags, piles, and boxes full of leftovers.

Grab your planner and set aside specific times to

- ▲ Make decisions about the "undecided" pile.

- ▲ Deliver articles you're donating to charity (or call to have them picked up).

- ▲ Take articles to the consignment shop.

- ▲ Deliver items you're giving (or returning) to friends and relatives.

- ▲ Have a garage sale (after you've organized the whole house).

- ▲ Drop off items to be dry-cleaned, mended, or altered.

Set aside a day or two to

▲ Catch up on laundry.

▲ Catch up on mending.

▲ Catch up on ironing.

▲ Go shopping for accessories or pieces you need to complete an outfit.

I suggest sending your family to a nudist colony for the week so that you can get *completely* caught up!

Step 7: Set Up Systems for the Future

Getting caught up is just the first step. To stay on top of laundry chores and mending, you need to set up systems. Our grandmothers washed on Monday, ironed on Tuesday, and cleaned on Wednesday. Maybe they were onto something. Here are a few tips to help you get organized.

▲ **Dry cleaning.** Designate a special place and container for everyone's dry cleaning. Maybe another family member could be responsible for taking and picking up dry cleaning on a specific day each week or every other week. Note on your planner when the dry cleaning is to be ready for pickup so that you don't forget it.

▲ **Laundry.** (First, teach laundry skills to all family members over the age of 10.) Set aside a particular day or days to do your laundry. Place a basket or hamper in each bedroom for dirty clothes, and designate a different receptacle (a basket or mesh bag) for hand washables so that they don't get mixed up with the machine washables. Do laundry in a logical sequence. For example, start with the loads that are the most difficult to put away and the ones with articles that require ironing. Do your ironing while you're waiting for the other loads to finish. Set the timer when you start a load so that you'll be ready when it's finished to put in another load right away. The longer clothing sits in the washer or the dryer, the worse it wrinkles. It's easier to press or iron clothes that aren't overdried.

▲ **Ironing.** Have a plan for clothes that need ironing. Put ironing in a clear plastic bag, an open basket, or a mesh bag so that you can easily see what's there. If you really hate ironing or don't have the time for it, pay someone to do it. Other choices include wearing only terrycloth or going for the wrinkled look.

▲ **Sewing.** Put together a small sewing kit that includes scissors, thread in basic colors, needles, pins, and a small pincushion, plus a small box containing buttons that need to be reattached (not your whole button collection). Put these in a mending basket next to your TV-watching chair or phone, or take it to your mother's house when you visit her.

Summary of Important Clothing-Storage Points

▲ Have a master plan; don't just do a closet-by-closet cleanup.

▲ Make decisions about what to keep and what not to keep.

▲ Take everything out of closets and drawers (one closet or dresser at a time) before putting things back.

▲ Put away only things you can and will wear now.

▲ Put away articles one at a time.

▲ Be determined to have laundry and ironing completely caught up on a weekly basis, mending on a monthly basis.

You may need to adjust your master plan from time to time. That's okay. But if you deviate from it, readjust it before you continue.

Checklist: What You Learned

This chapter showed you how to do the following things:

- ❏ Categorize clothing.
- ❏ Choose storage locations for various types of clothing.
- ❏ Design storage plans for each area.
- ❏ Find or buy containers and supplies.
- ❏ Empty each closet, drawer, and area.
- ❏ Sort all clothing and accessories.
- ❏ Put away clothing and accessories only if they are currently wearable.
- ❏ Buy, mend, and repair items to update your wardrobe.
- ❏ Get rid of what you do not want.
- ❏ Catch up on mending, sewing, and laundry.
- ❏ Set up systems to remain caught up.

Organizing your clothing and accessories will yield great rewards. Getting dressed, caring for clothes, and finding what you need will take less time than it used to. You'll save money by rediscovering and refurbishing clothes you already own. Saving space will give your clothes room to breathe; they'll last longer and you'll look better. And saving your sanity means you can proceed to chapter 6 and start organizing your papers.

The Paper Chase: Creating Files from Piles

Papers of one sort or another creep into our homes on a daily basis. They collect everywhere and can be found in all rooms, in most drawers, on dressers, between magazines, and under refrigerator magnets. They are tacked on walls and stuffed in baskets. That's okay, if you don't have to…

▲ Spend four hours looking for your children's health records every year when they go to camp…

▲ Locate the warranty on the broken toaster you bought four months ago…

▲ Rely on your memory for credit-card companies to call—and their phone numbers—when you lose your wallet.

Papers come to us in all

Size, SHAPES, COLORS, TEXTURES

Papers also have various

levels of importance

When I say "papers," I mean newspapers, junk mail, bills, letters, wedding invitations, school papers, magazine articles, bulletins, flyers, photos, notices, maps, and marriage licenses. All these items must be read, answered, filled out, paid, filed, returned, tossed out, or taken to a safe-deposit box. Each piece should have a place to go so it doesn't create clutter or get lost, torn, or mutilated.

The simple five-step system in this chapter will help you end the paper chase. Specifically, you will learn

▲ To gather and sort all papers in your home.

▲ To set up an efficient storage system for financial matters, household and family business, and personal papers.

▲ To set up working files for financial matters, household and family business, and personal papers.

▲ To organize photographs and other memorabilia.

▲ To store important papers in a safe place.

Paper Measure: Ways to Reduce Your Daily Dose of Junk Mail

▲ *Write to the Direct Marketing Association Preference Service, P.O. Box 9008, Farmingdale, NY 11735-9008. Tell them to remove your name from unsolicited junk mailing lists. It takes about three months to kick in.*

▲ *When ordering online and from mail-order companies, insist that they not sell, rent, or give your name to any other company.*

▲ *Write to companies asking that your name be removed from their mailing lists.*

▲ *Cancel subscriptions to periodicals you don't read.*

▲ *If you receive unwanted catalogs, call the senders' 800 numbers and ask to be removed from their distribution lists. Catalogs are like cockroaches; when one appears, you know there are thousands more nearby.*

▲ *Do not fill out the part of product registration/warranty cards that asks about your interests, unless you want mail.*

▲ *Return unwanted mail in the sender's postage-paid envelope.*

▲ *Write "refused; return to sender" and put the piece back in the mailbox.*

Barbara Hemphill's book *Taming the Paper Tiger* is an excellent paper-organizing tool. There are also software packages that can help you organize your papers.

Step 1: Gather Your Papers While You May

Find some open space in your home that you can occupy for a few days while you sort and decide what kinds of storage you need. Your work area can be a huge table with other tables nearby, a king-size bed you won't be needing for a while, a regulation-size Ping-Pong table, or a whole room!

You'll be making at least three big piles of papers, then dividing and subdividing them into smaller and smaller piles, so allow plenty of room to spread out. Round up a few trash bags, a paper shredder (if you have one), and some file folders and shallow boxes or box lids for sorting purposes.

Set Up Categories

Make three big signs: "Financial Matters," "Household and Family Business," and "Memorabilia." Add two more signs if you wish: "Other" and "Supplies." Here's an explanation of each category:

▲ **Financial Matters** (Fin): Any papers that concern banking, bills, loans, insurance, budgets, investments, taxes, credit cards, and mortgages.

▲ **Household and Family Business** (HFB): Nonfinancial items such as titles, warranties, pending business and invitations, important phone numbers, and informational or interesting reference materials–which could include recipes, shopping lists, hints and tips, travel information, product instructions, clippings, and reminders about things you "saw just the other day and can't remember where." Well, now you can remember.

▲ **Memorabilia** (M): Reminders of people and past (not upcoming) events. Some memorabilia items–wedding invitations, for example–may start out as "Household and Family Business" and become "Memorabilia" when they require no further action.

▲ You might want a fourth area labeled **Other** for papers that don't seem to fit into the Big Three, such as job-related papers you've brought home from work or papers relating to a hobby (such as genealogy).

▲ **Supplies** (S) might make a fifth pile if you have a lot of blank checks, blank envelopes, letter paper, notepads, fax paper, unused greeting cards, labels, transparencies, and other clean paper goods scattered around.

Place the signs in the area you plan to use for sorting. Brew a pot of tea and put on your favorite CD, and you're ready to begin.

Start Gathering

Gather all your personal and household papers from around your home, your office, and your cars (don't forget the glove compartments). Don't forget those hiding in your drawers, files, magazine stacks, and bathroom cupboards. If you have a file cabinet, empty it. Empty your safe-deposit box or make copies of the contents and list them, along with pertinent information such as serial numbers and monetary values. As you collect your papers, deposit them in the appropriate area. If you can't decide where they go, put them in the "Other" pile for now.

Make your stacks neat, but don't try to sort things into subcategories at this point. It might be helpful to place baskets or boxes in your sorting areas for small receipts, sticky notes, and other papers that might otherwise get lost.

Papers to Gather

Here are some things to look for, along with the categories they should go into:

School papers (M)

Letters from friends that don't require an answer (M)

Greeting cards you've received (M)

Greeting cards to be sent (S)

Photographs (M)

Travel brochures (HFB)

Camp information for the kids (HFB)

Magazine and newspaper articles of interest (M or HFB)

Invitations received (M or HFB)

Marriage license (HFB)

Diplomas (HFB)

To-do lists (HFB or Other)

Mysterious scraps of paper (Other)

Warranties and product registrations (HFB)

Instruction booklets and sheets (HFB)

Maps (HFB)

Bills to be paid (Fin)

Bills that have been paid (Fin)

Pamphlets (M, HFB, Fin, or Other)

Income-tax information (Fin)

Appliance brochures (HFB)

Home-improvement items (HFB)

Blank checks (S)

(continues)

(continued)

Canceled checks (Fin)

Birth certificates (HFB)

Insurance policies (HFB or Fin)

Telephone lists for school, bridge group, and so on (HFB)

Pictures to be framed (M or HFB)

Health records (HFB)

Car papers (HFB)

Claim checks for laundry, photos, and so on (HFB)

Wills (HFB)

Decorating ideas (HFB)

Papers for volunteer work (HFB)

Schedules for softball games, dance club, and so on (HFB)

Things in your wallets and purses (M, HFB, or Fin)

Job-related documents (Other)

Unused envelopes (S)

_____

_____

_____

_____

Step 2: Divide and Conquer (Big Piles)

Begin sorting the three "big piles" (Financial Matters, Household and Family Business, and Memorabilia) into smaller piles representing subcategories under the Big Three. We've suggested possible subcategories for each category in the following sections; you may have others to add as well. Make small signs for each subcategory so you remember what you are putting where. As suggested earlier, put your job-related papers in the "Other" pile.

Subcategories for Financial Matters (Fin)

Canceled checks, bank statements, insurance policies, insurance claim forms, insurance payment records, receipts, paid bills, unpaid bills, loan coupon books, budgets, stocks, bonds, tax records, credit-card information, savings passbooks, and loan records.

Subcategories for Household and Family Business (HFB)

Car titles, product brochures and warranties (appliances, toys, jewelry, and so on), home-improvement information, pending invitations, decorating information, letters to be answered, forms to fill out, family health records, pet records and information, licenses, birth certificates, funeral plans, wills, claim checks for repairs and services, how-to articles, travel brochures, camp information, passports, diplomas, lotto tickets, service agreements, symphony rosters, team rosters, poison and first-aid emergency information, and eyeglass prescriptions.

Subcategories for Memorabilia (M)

Schoolwork, correspondence, souvenirs, photos and negatives, news articles, artwork, family history, and your sister's poems.

Step 3: Subdivide and Reconquer (Small Piles)

In step 1, you put all your papers into four or five piles. In step 2, you separated the three big piles into subcategories. Now, one item at a time, divide each of the subcategory piles into several smaller piles. If you have clear boxes or file folders, you may want to place the papers in them. In this step, you will probably want to subdivide by time period in many instances; that is, arrange items in chronological order.

Financial Matters Sub-Subcategories

Keep current income-tax–related items separate from older receipts and other papers, possibly categorized by type of income or expense. Here are suggestions for sub-subcategories:

1. Insurance, retirement, annuities, and so on
    a. Claims
    b. Policies
    c. Statements
2. Income tax
    a. Past years
    b. Current year
        (1) Receipts
        (2) Forms
        (3) Instructions and booklets
3. Bills
    a. Paid
    b. Unpaid

4. Checking account(s) (keep accounts separate)

   a. Reconciled statements

   b. Canceled checks

   c. Bank information and policies, PIN numbers

5. Savings account(s)

6. Stocks and bonds

7. Budget

8. Articles concerning finances

9. Supplies

   a. Blank checks

   b. Blank balance sheets

   c. Blank check registers

Household and Family Business Sub-Subcategories

You can go one of two ways. Actually, you'll probably go both ways: classifying some items by family member and others by subject or type. For instance, you might have a "health" category for articles but keep each person's health records with their birth certificates and other personal records. Or you might post an article about teenage acne and good eating habits prominently on the refrigerator and later store it with the health articles.

Instead of storing sports and school schedules by the individual they apply to (see item 2-c in the following list), you might find a "current schedules" subcategory more helpful. The following are only suggestions. Use the classification system that suits you and your family.

1. Health

   a. Reference articles

   b. Individual health records

2. Individual records

   a. Birth certificates

   b. Current school papers

   c. Schedules (softball games, bridge, PTA)

   d. Diplomas, honors, awards

   e. Employment records

   f. Health records

   g. Copies of things in your wallet

   h. Copy of your will (keep the original in your safe-deposit box)

   i. Marriage license

3. Social

   a. Invitations

   b. Address/phone lists

   c. Rosters and schedules

4. Volunteer organizations (sort by organization)

   a. Minutes

   b. Business

5. House and home maintenance

   a. Decorating articles

   b. Pictures to be framed

   c. Phone/address list of repair people

   d. Cleaning tips

   e. Home-improvement receipts

   f. Appliance warranties

   g. Appliance brochures–large appliances

    h. Appliance brochures–small appliances

    i. Maintenance history and schedules

    j. Deed

    k. Inspection records

6. Automobile

    a. Title

    b. Registration

    c. Insurance (or place under "Financial Matters"–or copy it and keep it both places)

    d. Repair records

    e. Auto club information

    f. Maintenance schedule

7. Pets

    a. Registration papers

    b. Veterinary records

    c. Obedience school diploma

    d. Articles, brochures

    e. Pedigrees

8. Entertainment

    a. Schedules for dance club

    b. Menus from favorite restaurants

    c. Brochures

9. Travel

    a. Itineraries

    b. Maps and guides

    c. Mileage logs

    d. Frequent-flyer information

    e. Tickets

10. Food

    a. Recipes

    b. Menus

    c. Articles and nutrition information

11. Clothing

    a. Laundering instructions

    b. Fashion articles and pictures

    c. Pamphlet on "50 ways to tie a scarf"

12. Errands, claim checks, and receipts for

    a. Photographs being developed

    b. Shoes being repaired

    c. Clothes being dry-cleaned

    d. Watches, jewelry being repaired

13. Miscellaneous

    a. Articles of interest, humor, and so on

    b. Reference materials

14. Supplies

    a. Blank greeting cards, postcards

    b. Envelopes, stamps

    c. Stationery

Memorabilia Sub-Subcategories

1. Photos and negatives

2. Family history

3. Schoolwork, writing, certificates, diplomas, honors, news articles, letters

    a. Parents', grandparents'

    b. Yours

    c. Spouse's

    d. Children's

4. Old cards, letters

5. Social mementos (invitations, programs, show tickets)

6. Scrapbooks

When you start actually *storing* the items you're now *sorting,* you may want to keep other memorabilia with or near the paper memorabilia in a trunk or file cabinet, depending on size. "Other" memorabilia might include T-shirts, dried flowers, commemorative mugs, or a jar of sand from your Hawaiian honeymoon.

Step 4: Sort and Store According to Amount of Use

When storing papers, it's important to separate those that are (1) used and rarely referred to from those that are (2) occasionally or (3) often used, and those that (4) require immediate attention.

Establish at least four storage levels:

1. Rarely referred to
   = deep storage

2. Sometimes referred to
   = occasional reference

3. Often referred to
   = ready reference

4. Immediate attention
   = desktop to-do
   = desktop pending

Now examine each pile, determine how often the items are used or referred to, and decide where and how to store them.

Level One: Deep Storage

If an item is never or rarely used (once a year or less), place it in deep storage. A level-one storage place could be a file cabinet in the basement, a safe-deposit box, or a trunk in the attic—somewhere that's not impossible to get to, but where you won't trip over it every day.

Consider a safe-deposit box for official papers such as licenses, contracts, certificates, policies, titles, passports, and wills. Find safe, fireproof storage for all valuable and irreplaceable documents. Ask yourself what would happen if a paper were lost, burned, or stolen. If the loss would be traumatic, it's a good idea to store the item in a safe-deposit box or a fireproof, bulletproof, childproof security chest or file cabinet. You might want to make copies of items that you need to refer to and put the copies in a more handy storage area.

Level Two: Occasional Reference

Occasional-reference storage is for papers you refer to once or twice a year, not monthly or more. They should be fairly easy to get to. Place them in file cabinets or filing crates, or on shelves located in a convenient but out-of-the-way area. If you use a file cabinet for level-two financial, family/home business, and memorabilia items, place them in separate, clearly labeled drawers and color-coded files.

Level Three: Ready Reference

Ready-reference storage is for papers you will likely add to, act on, or refer to monthly or more often, such as receipts for tax-deductible or home-improvement items, current bills, and bank statements to be reconciled.

Ready-reference places should be accessible and easy to find, in a spot you pass by at least daily, and near where you sort your mail—ideally in your office area. Storage might be on open shelves or in open filing crates, clear-plastic boxes, or open file trays. (Do you see a common thread here? You need to be able to see what you have got.) Other possibilities are clear-plastic photo holders, recipe files, photo albums, bulletin boards, and briefcases. A sturdy, clear-plastic zipper bag or small clipboard is useful in the glove compartment for your vehicle registration and insurance card.

A great ready-reference container for photographs is a clear-plastic photo organizer. You can organize 500 photos in about an hour…unless you get swept away by the memories. Photos are arranged in groups. Although the photos are not quite as secure as in photo albums, they're much easier to work with. You can add to a group without rearranging pages or using glue, paste, photo corners, or staples. As a bonus, these organizers have compartments just for negatives.

Here's how to store photos in plastic photo organizers:

▲ Decide how to arrange them. Do you want a section for each family member, or for each year, or for each pet, or for each occasion…? Because we have so many photos, one of my photo organizers has a section for Susie, one for Jimmy, one for Susie and Jimmy together, one for Dad and Susie, and so on. We have such a photogenic dog that we could eventually have separate sections on Bernie sleeping, Bernie eating, and Bernie just being cute. Your arrangements will depend on your activities and interests. Maybe you'll want one or more organizers just for travel, with sections for the 1992 trip to California, the 2000 trip to the Orange Bowl, and last year's Mediterranean cruise.

▲ Sort photos into piles according to the categories you've selected.

▲ Label each section of the plastic container (labels are included).

▲ Put the photos in the proper sections.

Level Four: Desktop Reference

Desktop-reference items need immediate or prompt attention or follow-up. They should be quickly accessible on your desk, in your planner or briefcase, or on a bulletin board or refrigerator. You might have designated areas on bulletin boards and in briefcases for level-three and level-four items. One side of your refrigerator door might hold a list of frequently called phone numbers (level three–ready reference), the other a shopping list (level four–desktop).

The object is for the papers to be visible and organized, whether they're in file folders, letter trays, or piles. A message center or communication center should be located on or near the desktop for others' messages and mail.

Desktop reference includes both desktop to-do and desktop pending. Desktop to-do items need to be dealt with now, if not sooner: forms to fill out, letters to answer, dog licenses to renew, invitations to send, sweepstakes to enter, recipes to be sent for the church cookbook, items to add to your planner, or bank statements to reconcile. Papers to file or put in a scrapbook are also to-do items.

Desktop-pending items are tasks you can't complete until a certain date or until someone else acts. For instance, if you're collecting checks from members of your dance club so that you can make dinner reservations, you might put checks received into a pending file until you've collected from everyone, or until the deadline. Mark your planner for a few days before the deadline so that you will get the reservations and checks in the mail on time. Other items might include refunds for rebate forms you have sent in, sweepstakes you've entered, claim checks for dry cleaning and shoe repair, or film-development reminders–generally, anything you need to follow up on in the near future.

You can separate and store pending items in piles, in file trays, in slotted mail racks, in your planner, in your briefcase, or on a bulletin board. Generally, all pending items should be together. If you place pending items on your bulletin board, make sure they're in plain view, easy to reach, and not mixed with unimportant items. Keep them separate from desktop to-do items in plain sight or close at hand so that you don't forget them.

You'll find detailed instructions for setting up your desktop in chapter 7.

Step 5: Set Up Filing Systems

With a well-designed file system, you can store and retrieve papers in seconds! Here are some general filing suggestions and an example filing arrangement.

Some General Suggestions

Containers for file folders can range from large four- or five-drawer file cabinets to small filing crates. They can be cardboard, plastic, or steel. The same types of storage, appropriately located, might be suitable for various levels. Filing crates, for example, might work fine for occasional-reference, ready-reference, or desktop items.

Color-coding your file folders is ideal for easy filing and retrieval. You might, for instance, assign a different color to each family member *or* (not *and*) each subject area–for example, green (as in money) for financial files, blue for memorabilia, yellow for appliances, pink for health records, and red for auto information.

Hanging file folders, such as those made by Smead or Sparco, are easy to work with. They are sturdy and they move easily in filing crates and drawers. You can use them alone or to hold other (non-hanging) folders, preferably the same color. Thus, your red hanging file, labeled "Family Car" could hold red file folders labeled "Repair Receipts," "Brochures," and "Maintenance Charts." Label all file folders in a way that's easy to read and reflects the contents as accurately as possible.

For the most efficient filing system, your individual folders should be one-half to one inch thick when filled. Thinner files you probably won't add much to might be consolidated with similar files. It's better, though, for files to be too thin than too thick.

If you can't read the label when the file is in the cabinet, the folder is too thick. Divide the contents into separate folders. For example, replace a folder overflowing with appliance brochures, making new folders for (1) large appliances and (2) small appliances, or (1) kitchen appliances and (2) non-kitchen appliances, or (1) appliances–warranties and (2) appliances–directions for use.

Place small papers–receipts, wallet-size cards, and so on–in clear sheet protectors or tape them to letter-size paper, so they won't be lost, overlooked, or crushed in the folder.

Another way to subdivide files is alphabetically (A–J, K–Q, R–Z) or chronologically: (1980–1989, 1990–1999, 2000–present).

An Example Filing Arrangement

Here is an example of a color-coded ready-reference filing arrangement:

A. Blue folders: Family

   One hanging file for each family member; a hanging file might contain separate folders for

   1. Health records

   2. Resumes

   3. Grade reports

   4. Social Security card, birth certificate, and will (copies)

   5. Other

B. Red folders: Transportation

   One hanging file for each vehicle.

   1. Warranty information

   2. Repair records

   3. Brochures

   4. Other

C. Yellow folders: Insurance

   1. Insurance policies (separate by type)

   2. Insurance forms (separate by type)

   3. Insurance claims and settlements

D. Green folders: Financial

   1. Budget

   2. Tax-deductible receipts for the current year

   3. Savings account information

   4. Paid bills

   5. This year's bank statements

   6. Investments

E. Orange folders: Household

    1. Home-improvement records

    2. Large indoor appliances: warranties and brochures

    3. Small indoor appliances: warranties and brochures

    4. Outdoor appliances and equipment

    5. Household inventory

F. White folders: Miscellaneous

    1. Pets

    2. Current projects

    3. Items of interest, humor, and so on

    4. Miscellaneous phone lists

    5. Volunteer organizations (separate files for each organization)

Memorabilia for Display or Gift-Giving

▲ *Place a collage of artwork or photos in a picture frame.*

▲ *Have photos enlarged at a copy store.*

▲ *Make postcards of a favorite photo.*

▲ *Have a photo put on a T-shirt or coffee mug.*

▲ *Make a jigsaw puzzle out of a photo or art project.*

▲ *Decorate your home with children's artwork.*

▲ *Make shadow boxes to hold medals, baby shoes, or other small family treasures.*

You've Caught Your Papers in Your Paper Chase!

If you've completed all the steps, adapting them to your situation when necessary, your paper storage might look something like this:

▲ Desktop and pending items on your desktop or workspace, or on a shelf within arm's reach of your desk chair.

▲ Ready reference in a file drawer or filing crate near your workspace or desk.

▲ Occasional reference in file cabinets or file boxes in an accessible area.

▲ Deep storage in a storeroom, basement (if not too damp), or other remote area.

Checklist: What You Learned

This chapter showed you how to do the following things:

❏ Sort all papers into five categories—the Big Three plus "Other" and paper supplies.

❏ Refine and subdivide your categories.

❏ Designate levels of storage.

❏ Set up a filing system.

❏ Store papers.

❏ Organize photos.

You may also want to

❏ Update scrapbooks, albums, or files.

❏ Set up a system for mail handling.

❏ Create displays of children's work.

If you have completed this checklist, it's time for you to set up your office and establish systems that allow you to stay on top of your papers...not under them. Chapter 7 shows you how.

Part III

Organizing Your Household

An Office in Every Home

Most of us have financial, legal, family, personal, and household business that we conduct from our homes. For these responsibilities we need a special place to work and to keep our records and supplies—a family office, which I discuss in the first part of this chapter. More and more of us are also setting up professional offices at home, expanding an existing family office, or setting up a separate business office. The second part of this chapter deals with home business offices.

In this chapter, I'll use the term *family office* when referring to the place you take care of personal and household business. For the professional office in the home—used to operate your own enterprise or do work for your employer—I'll use the term *home business office* or *business office*. Both are legitimately called "home offices," but I make the distinction so you won't be tripping over the vocabulary as you read.

On the Home Front: Family Offices

Every home needs an office because everyone has bills to pay, letters to write, and manuals to read. Even if you live alone in an apartment, you have responsibility for your livelihood, health, personal growth, rent, maintenance, upkeep, belongings, affiliations, and transportation. If you live in a 36-room mansion with your spouse, Great Uncle Bowen, and eight children, you may have several additional responsibilities. Both situations, and all those in between, require some type of office setup.

Your family office–the place where you handle household and family business and finances–can be in a closet or a large room, or it can consist of a countertop and file cabinet. Small or large, plain or fancy, it should be in a specific and exclusive location. Because your office will also be a communication center for the rest of your household, it should be centrally or otherwise conveniently located.

You'll use your office for paying bills, filling out registration forms, planning menus, making calls for Girl Scout cookie sales, planning a Heart Association fund-raiser, sketching fall fashions for the hottest French designer, retrieving

appliance instructions, preparing blueprints for your next mansion, referring to health records, answering invitations, planning your week, and phoning service technicians.

Your office is where you'll keep desktop pending and desktop to-do papers, ready-reference items, and–if you have enough space–occasional-reference storage. Be sure the categories are clearly separated and appropriately accessible (see chapter 6).

This chapter will enable you to

▲ Find a good location for your office.

▲ Find furnishings and supplies for your office.

▲ Set up your office.

▲ Establish a communication center that family members will use routinely.

▲ Set up your desktop area.

▲ Set up systems for handling business.

Step 1: Locate a Spot for Your Family Office

When deciding where to put an office, consider these issues:

▲ Floor space for a desk, file cabinets, and a chair

▲ Available space for supplies and equipment

▲ Wall space for shelves, bulletin boards, hooks, pegboard, or wire-mesh racks

▲ Lighting

▲ Access to phone lines

▲ Access to and number of electrical outlets

▲ Accessibility to other household members

Your office needs to be large enough to fulfill your needs. If you have (or plan to get) lots of office equipment, you'll need more space than if you have little. (Allow room for additional equipment, such as a scanner, an external disk drive, and other peripherals. New technology is flooding the market and is quickly becoming affordable.) If you use numerous working files or reference files, you'll need space for file cabinets. You can use wall space for some supplies and equipment by using shelving.

Step 2: Supply Your Family Office

Certain supplies and equipment are essential. You can gather some things from around your home and buy others as the need arises. Make sure that your supplies have a special place, that they stay in your office area, and that they're conveniently located.

Furniture and Accessories Every Office Should Have

As you gather or purchase each item, check it off the following list:

_____ Desk with drawers, or a sturdy counter resting on two two-drawer file cabinets

_____ Telephone (cordless or with a long cord for convenience)

_____ Good lighting

_____ Calculator (any size, depending on your needs)

_____ File cabinet

_____ Filing crate

_____ Bulletin board, cork or magnetized

_____ Wastebasket

(continues)

(continued)

It would be great to have

_____ Typewriter or a computer

_____ Printer

_____ Scanner

_____ Fax machine

_____ Copier

_____ Answering machine

_____ Clock or clock-radio

_____ Tape recorder

Paper Goods to Keep in Stock

_____ Blank envelopes

_____ Stamps (you can buy them online or by mail; ask your letter carrier)

_____ Notebook paper

_____ Unused checkbooks and check recorders

_____ Bank reconciliation sheet

_____ Telephone book

_____ ZIP code directory

_____ Dictionary and synonym finder; other reference books

_____ Scratch paper

_____ Stationery

_____ 3 × 5 or 4 × 6 cards

_____ Thank-you notes

_____ Prestamped postal cards

_____ Extra greeting cards: birthday, wedding, sympathy, new baby, anniversary, holidays, miscellaneous

_____ Self-stick notes of various sizes and colors

Office Supplies to Have on Hand

_____ Computer disks, labels, paper

_____ Pens that work

_____ Sharpened pencils

_____ Pencil sharpener

_____ Correction fluid (now in "dry" dispensers)

_____ Glue (bottles or stick, permanent or removable)

_____ Three-ring binders

_____ Push pins or thumbtacks

_____ Trays for pens, pencils, paper clips, and other small supplies

_____ Eraser

_____ Stapler

_____ Staples

_____ Staple remover

_____ Clear tape and tape dispenser

_____ Scissors

_____ Permanent markers

_____ Highlighters

_____ Clamps and paper clips: large and small

_____ Paper punch (a three-hole punch is especially handy)

_____ Colored file folders

_____ Colored hanging file olders

_____ Three or four stackable trays

_____ Toner or ink cartridges for printers

Get the Light Right!

Good lighting is important! Sunlight is preferable; but natural-spectrum bulbs also improve mood and alertness. Compact fluorescent bulbs are economical and cooler than incandescent bulbs. The newer fluorescent bulbs don't flicker (or cause headaches) like the old ones. Direct lighting is preferable to overhead.

Position lamps and computers in a way that avoids glare. Wall color is also a factor...it takes more electricity to light a room with dark walls. Wall color can also affect glare, mood, and productivity, so choose your office wall colors carefully.

Step 3: Set Up Your Family Office

First, remove from your present or future office space any items that aren't conducive to home and family administration. Then bring in what you need and put everything in its place. Put up lights, arrange furniture, and place accessories where they're most advantageous. If you have a typewriter or computer, make sure there's enough working space beside it for your notes and references. See step 4 for instructions on setting up your family communication center.

Keep Important Items Close at Hand

Think in terms of concentric circles when organizing your workspace. With your chair at the center, the innermost circle should contain essential items you use most often, such as the phone, your computer or drawing board, note paper and pens, frequently used reference books and files, computer disks, stamps, a stapler, a wastebasket, and so forth. You should be able to reach anything within this circle without leaving your chair.

The next circle should include items you use less often—maybe your copier, filing crate, paper punch, and extra pens. They may be on shelves or behind you on another desk or cabinet. You may need to turn around or stand up to reach these. To reach things in the third circle, you might have to leave your chair and walk a few steps. This circle could contain samples, some books and files, and equipment.

In general, the less you have to stand up and move around, the better your concentration will be. On the other hand, everyone needs to stretch and walk around at regular intervals—at least every two hours. So don't forget to give yourself a break!

If you haven't done so, arrange your files according to the instructions in chapter 6, storing ready-reference and (if there's room) occasional-reference files in your office. I will discuss desktop-reference items in step 5.

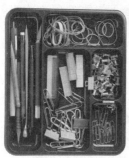 Your desk drawers—not including file drawers—should contain only supplies: pens, paper, clips, staples, note paper, blank greeting cards, and so forth. Any business items should be in your files, on your desk, or in your daily planner.

You'll save time by arranging your supplies according to how often you use them. If you don't use something in your office, put it somewhere else. Use drawer dividers or silverware trays to keep clips, scissors, pens, and other supplies compartmentalized so they're easy to put away and even easier to retrieve.

You should be able to see what you have without moving anything else (unless you want to hide something, of course). If you have little or no drawer space, put some supplies in containers hooked to wire grids on the wall or the back of a door, or use a plastic drawer unit on wheels.

Step 4: Set Up Your Home/Family Communication Center

Your office should be the designated family communication center—a central location for mail, phone numbers, reminders, telephone messages, dental-appointment cards, softball schedules, a family calendar, and lists for family chores and responsibilities, shopping, and errands—plus whatever else you need to keep everyone informed.

If your office is off the beaten path, the refrigerator or a strategically placed bulletin board might be a good place for the communication center. However humble it might be, you should keep your communication center up-to-date; otherwise, your family will soon start ignoring it. The communication center should also include a family calendar for activities and appointments (separate from your own planner) so everyone will be aware of everyone else's upcoming events.

An effective family calendar includes each family member's activities because they might affect someone else in the household. You may want family members to put their own color-coded messages on the family calendar (if their writing isn't too big or sloppy), or to write their commitments on sticky notes so you can add them to the family calendar. Be sure to attach a pen or pencil with Velcro to the family calendar or nearby.

In the same area, designate a spot for shopping lists, supplies needed, mail, and telephone messages. With some answering machines, you can leave messages for each other (and reminders for yourself) by using the "message" function.

Add a computer, and your communication center gains vast possibilities—from simply leaving electronic notes to using purchased or online organizing software. It's fairly inexpensive to network your family's computers, allowing you to share files (including an electronic copy of the family calendar) and send e-mail on your own family Internet.

Used consistently, your communication center will keep track of the family's activities, needs, wants, and ideas. A well-used communication center that effectively conveys family responsibilities, activities, and requests can prevent stress caused by misunderstanding, missed messages, or lost mail. It may take a little training or a few bribes to get people into the habit of checking the communication center regularly, but be patient and insistent. It will soon pay off and make everyone's life a bit easier.

Step 5: Set Up Your Family Office Desktop

When you have gathered your supplies and equipment, arranged your communication center, and organized your files, it's time to set up your desktop.

A functional desktop is not cluttered. It's too easy to lose things in clutter, and the things on your desk are, or should be, important items that need to be dealt with. For documents requiring action down the road, such as an income-tax form due in a few months, make a note in your planner and file the form. If you're afraid you'll forget where you put it, jot that down in your planner, too. Your desktop should be clear of decorative items unless they have a function. Put the kids' school pictures and Aunt Maxine's pearl-handled silent butler on a little shelf above the desk.

Look in office-supply catalogs or stores to see the kinds of desktop organizers that are available. There are stacking trays, vertical files (also called sorters), and combination units (some with compartments for pencils and paper clips). In plastic, individual trays and vertical dividers cost about a dollar each. More durable and attractive steel, wood, wicker, and mesh units can cost a little—or a lot—more.

 Use these desktop organizers to hold items that are pending or need attention, such as letters to answer, greeting cards to send, appliance warranties to fill out, bills to pay, bank statements to reconcile, and items to add to your planner. Put longer-term pending and to-do in file storage only after you note in your planner the date you need to retrieve them.

Go through your desktop items once a week and file, answer, pay, write, fill out, and mail things as needed. Keep other essentials on your desk such as a phone, stapler, pens, and a good lamp. Close by should be extra staples, a phone book, envelopes, stamps, and other supplies you use often.

You can keep receipts and claim checks for film, dry cleaning, and repairs on your bulletin board, although they might be handier in your wallet or clipped to your car visor. Note in your planner where your items—such as repaired shoes and clean laundry—are and when they'll be ready.

Step 6: Make Your Electronics and Other Equipment Work for You

Modern technology can save you time by giving you more information more quickly, streamlining your tasks, and allowing you to communicate with others instantly. You might find touchscreens, voice-activated computers, standalone Internet devices, or other Internet-access and telecommunication devices well worth the cost. An external Zip drive makes it easy to compress programs and other files and move them off your hard drive. To avoid losing important information in the event that your computer crashes, you can back up your entire hard drive on Zip disks.

Office Machines and Internet Services

Recent advances in technology have improved and accelerated how people communicate and make it easier to be organized:

▲ **Scanners** can copy documents into word-processing software for editing, and can convert pictures into graphics files for printing, transmitting, or posting on the Web.

▲ Small, single-page **copiers** are inexpensive, and they soon pay for themselves in time saved if the alternative is frequent trips to the copy center for small jobs. Fax machines and scanners also function as copiers.

▲ **Printers** are indispensable. Add a scanner, and you can make multiple black-and-white and color copies.

▲ **Fax machines, e-mail, three-way and conference calling,** and **wireless phones** (some with Internet and e-mail access) make global communication possible from almost anywhere.

▲ Become familiar with the **Internet** for shopping (most online vendors gift-wrap and mail), banking, getting directions, making travel plans, and sending greeting cards—for starters. There are thousands of services available online. (See "E-errands: Go Everywhere Without Leaving Home," in chapter 3.)

Organizing Your Technology

Although technology saves time, it usually generates more paper (though it was designed to do the opposite) and can overload your filing system. Here are some tips to keep in mind for keeping up with the extra information that technology generates:

▲ Learn what to save on your hard drive, what to back up on a disk, and what to print. Ask yourself if you really need a hard copy. Maybe backing up on a floppy disk will do the job.

▲ For ease in finding documents, give computer files and corresponding hard-copy files the same names, and color-code floppy disks accordingly.

▲ Hard drives quickly become cluttered with un- needed software. Use an uninstall program to delete software you no longer use. Before you buy or download a new program, or purchase an accessory, make sure your computer has enough drive space and memory, a fast enough processor, and the necessary hardware (ports, sound cards, video cards, and so on).

▲ To prevent viruses–which can render your computer useless–open only those e-mail messages you know to be safe. Be wary about opening at- tached files, even if the sender is someone you know. We've recently seen a rash of viruses that infect computers and send out e-mails to infect others. Install antivirus software and back up your important files frequently.

▲ If you are constantly on the go and do business in transit, personal digital assistants (PDAs) or hand-held organizers, laptops, wireless phones, and pagers give you flexibility.

▲ Wireless phones and pagers make it hard to "get away from it all." To avoid that dilemma, schedule personal time and turn off your equipment.

▲ Scams do occur on the Internet. Be wary. Check Better Business Bureaus and get references if you are unsure of a Web site. Personal and financial information you give when ordering products may not be protected. Be aware of your vulnerability. There are ways to order over the Internet without giving your credit-card number online.

▲ Too much information can result from e-mails and faxes. Although they can be time-savers, they can also generate more work, create more documents, require decisions, and demand immediate responses. The senders may expect you to be able to get back to them, and soon. Control your own time. Determine ahead of time what you will read based on the type of information and the source. For instance, you may want to eliminate all advertising or humorous pieces. Use your e-mail client's screening features.

▲ The availability of Internet resources—for education, games, shopping, and services—can be overwhelming, consuming time and money before you realize it. Set time and spending limits for yourself before you log on.

Questions to Ask Before You Buy a Computer

▲ *Where can I get service and support?*

Many companies have toll-free numbers that may give you access to free support, but more often simply refer you to toll numbers. Ask about support plans—what do they cost, what do they cover, and for how long? Is extended service available?

▲ *Will the computer support my needs?*

If you want Internet access only, consider an Internet-access device. If you need a full-featured computer, buy one that can operate the software you'll be using—spreadsheets, word-processing programs, entertainment and games, graphics, photos, e-commerce, desktop publishing, music, and so on. Do your research online (ZDNet and About.com are good places to start) or consult a computer professional or salesperson.

▲ *Is the computer compatible with software and peripherals I now own?*

▲ *Is it compatible with school computers?*

Your Family Office in Action

With your office efficiently arranged and supplied, you're ready for business. You can handle household and family concerns calmly and effectively—just like Leonard, Gladys, and Mary in these real-life situations:

Leonard's Ladder to Successful Organizing

Leonard has five stacking trays on his desk. In the top one are things that need immediate attention. In the second tray are matters he should deal with soon, but not immediately. The third tray holds pending items; the fourth, to-be-filed papers that he's already dealt with. And in the bottom tray are reference materials he uses continually, including a ZIP code directory and a list of computer shortcuts.

Leonard checks the top tray daily or every other day, trays two and three weekly, tray four monthly (or whenever it gets full), and tray five as needed. Good, Leonard!

When Gladys Receives a Bill

Gladys pays her bills on the 15th of the month. When she receives a utility bill or any other invoice not requiring immediate payment, she places it in tray two, "Bills to Pay," with the others. On the 15th, when she pays her bills, she writes the date and check number on the portions she keeps. Gladys knows that her job is not done until the bills are mailed, so after putting the "return" portions and checks in envelopes, addressing the ones that aren't preprinted, and attaching postage, she places them in the mailbox and checks later to make sure the mail carrier has taken them. Then she files her portion with her receipts except for uninsured medical bills, charitable contributions, and other tax-deductible items. These she places in the current year's income-tax file (ready reference). She also has separate "paid" files for her utility bills, home improvements, and other expenses she wants to keep track of for future reference. (Gladys would like to use online banking, but she wants to take her time researching various vendors and plans.) Good, Gladys!

When Mary Receives a Wedding Invitation

Mary loves going to weddings, so she is sure to write the time and place for the wedding in her planner as soon as she opens the invitation. She makes a note on her to-do list to buy a crystal vase and a card. Because she has good manners, she immediately sends a reply to the invitation. If she is uncertain whether she can go, she puts a note in her planner to reply in a week. Then she posts the invitation in the communication center for her family to see. After the wedding, she files the invitation in her memorabilia file.

Mary is careful not to waste time and effort. Sometimes she orders the gift online and has it wrapped and sent to the bride. If she goes out to buy the gift, she takes the address with her and has the store wrap and deliver or mail the package for her. To Mary, it's usually worth the extra expense. Smart, Mary!

Your Turn! Some Example Situations

Using the examples of Leonard, Gladys, and Mary, how would you deal with the following items? Think of the steps you would take, what you would write in your planner and to-do list, when you would consider the item dealt with, and where you would store it.

▲ A letter requiring an answer

▲ A letter not requiring an answer

▲ A trade journal with interesting and relevant articles

▲ A card with your plumber's new address and phone number

▲ A brochure on the new car you want to buy

▲ A contest entry blank

▲ A new-appliance warranty card

▲ A newspaper article about a good friend

▲ Your son's math test with an "A"

▲ Your son's math test with a "D"

▲ Your daughter's application and health card for camp

Update Your Office with Organizing Products

Organizing devices such as labelers, address systems, and containers for the home and office are sold at hardware, office supply, discount, grocery, and home stores, among others. New designs, greater variety, designer colors, and lower prices make these products especially tempting. Catalogs also show an array of containers, file cabinets, and office tools for the home.

Catalogs and Web sites where you can find lots of helpful organizing supplies include

▲ *OfficeMax,* *www.officemax.com*

▲ *Office Depot,* *www.officedepot.com*

▲ *Staples,* *www.staples.com*

▲ *The Container Store,* *www.containerstore.com*

▲ *Organize Everything,* *www.organize-everything.com*

▲ *Hold Everything,* *www.holdeverything.com*

▲ *Lillian Vernon,* *www.lillianvernon.com*

▲ *Archive Designs, Inc.* *(for large document filing and storage products),* *www.archivedesignsinc.com*

▲ *Bantex* *(for ring files, folders, binders, and other office products),* *www.bantex.com*

▲ *Folders USA* *(file folders, color-coded labels, open filing, shelving),* *www.foldersusa.com*

▲ *Filemate.com* *(hanging file folders, labeling systems, and software to organize home or office)*

Mind Your Own Business: Home Business Offices

It's common for many consultants, writers, copy editors, bookkeepers, and other free spirits to have their businesses in their homes. Now, others in the work force are joining the work-at-home movement: Internet entrepreneurs of all kinds, employees of virtual companies, and others who enjoy being at home and the convenience of working there. Outside salespeople were among the home-office pioneers, but now other types of employees, from managers to programmers to support staff, are pressuring their companies for permission to telecommute at least part of the time. Day-care providers, hairdressers, mechanics, and others with home-based enterprises need offices separate from their work and storage areas, as do direct-sales (Avon, Tupperware, Shaklee, USana, Longaberger, and so forth) and catalog vendors. (Working at home prevents you from using bad weather as an excuse for failing to show up for work. If you're really organized, however, you can declare a "snow day" once in a while and spend the day in bed watching Alfred Hitchcock movies.)

The Voice of Experience

Consider this advice from veteran home-based workers:

▲ *Working at home is not a substitute for child care. Unless your enterprise is a casual undertaking, you'll need work time (and space) distinct from family time (and space). Meanwhile, even older kids need some supervision. Make whatever arrangements are necessary to free yourself from distractions—and guilt.*

▲ *Callers, visitors, and family members are likely to take advantage of you if you don't take a stand. Consider a separate phone line or (much cheaper) a custom-ringing phone number, which you answer during office hours. Make it clear to your family that you're not available for their transportation or errands, except by special arrangement—in advance. Close your office door.*

(continues)

(continued)

▲ *Log your time and car mileage and keep other records and receipts for income-tax purposes. In general, you're eligible for the home-office deduction if the home is your principal business location and if there is an area (it needn't be an entire room) used exclusively for business.*

▲ *Schedule regular outings—lunch with friends, professional meetings, club events—to network, keep current on developments in your field, and ward off feelings of isolation.*

First Things First

In the first part of this chapter, I addressed setting up an office for running your home. Setting up an office for running your business requires following and expanding on steps 1 through 5 in that section. We will return to those five steps using additional information on the following pages. But first, there are a few things you need to do that are specific to setting up a home business office:

▲ Research laws, ordinances, deed restrictions, and other limitations that might apply to your business and location. These can exist at the federal, state, county, municipal, and neighborhood levels.

▲ In all likelihood—especially if clients or customers come to your home—you'll need a liability rider or separate policy, and possibly separate coverage for business equipment and inventory. Ask your homeowners' or rental insurance agent.

▲ Determine whether you will want to "outsource" any of your business responsibilities.

Research Restrictions

When you dream about having your own home-based business, this task probably doesn't enter the picture, although it's an essential first step. The best place to start is the nearest Small Business Development Center or Service Corps of Retired Executives (SCORE) office. Commissioned by the Small Business Administration, these agencies are located nationwide, often at community colleges and universities. (You'll find more information at www.sba.gov.) Other good resources are trade associations (especially local chapters) and your local or state home-based business association. Converse with the experts at those offices and obtain printed material. Be a nuisance; ask lots of questions about qualifications, stipulations, laws, regulations, insurance, permits, and restrictions. You wouldn't want to spend months setting up Fido's Paw-Nail Clipping Parlor only to discover that you're not properly zoned.

Assess Your Needs and Responsibilities

Before you set up your office, you need to know what will occur there. Perhaps you will be doing some or all of the following:

▲ Handling correspondence

▲ Billing

▲ Bookkeeping

▲ Working with financial records and reports

▲ Mailing (and *bulk* mailing)

▲ Desktop publishing

▲ Creating artwork or graphics

▲ Marketing your business

▲ Keeping track of prospects

▲ Storing inventory

▲ Storing product samples

▲ Holding conferences or meetings

▲ Seeing clients

▲ Creating a product

▲ Providing space and equipment for employees

Each of these responsibilities entails different requirements for space, equipment, supplies, and expertise. If employees or clients will be coming to your home, for example, assess the need for wheelchair accessibility for customers or employees.

Determine What to Outsource

Outsource means "I don't have time, I don't have space, I don't have the right equipment, and besides I don't know how." Recognize that you can't do everything yourself. Even if you could, other businesses can often provide services for you in ways that are better or less expensive. If you make more per hour than it would cost you to pay an "outsourcer" (or would that be "outsourcerer"?), then your time is usually better spent earning money. At the very least, you should do some outsourcing right off the bat: Consult a lawyer (even if you've done your research), and check with an accountant about possible forms of organization (sole proprietorship and various types of partnerships and corporations).

Other outsourcing possibilities include bookkeeping, payroll, marketing, secretarial work, data entry, mailings, prospect tracking, and business-plan development. Consider these possibilities as you're budgeting your time.

Five Steps to Setting Up a Business Office in Your Home

Now that you've researched, assessed, and outsourced, it's time to follow the five steps for setting up a home office, which are based on the steps for setting up a family office that were discussed earlier in this chapter. Keep in mind that you'll need more and different supplies, equipment, and workspaces for your home business office than for your family office.

Step 1: Locate a Spot for Your Business Office

Ideally, your home business will not double as a guest room, storeroom, or pantry—or as a family office. If you must share it with nonbusiness activities, keep business-related items in a separate part of the room. Label them clearly and use them only for business. (See step 5, later in this chapter, for ways to separate household and business desktop items.)

Find an area large enough for your workspace, equipment, and storage needs. Make sure there are enough outlets and phone jacks; consider customer access, seating, and a waiting area. The area should be far enough away from your gurgling baby and the family's pinball machine that you can sound professional over the phone, but not so far away that you feel like you're in solitary confinement.

If your business requires a woodworking area, kitchen, greenhouse, garage, or darkroom, your choices of where to locate your office are limited. In any case, your office should be as close to these working areas as possible. After finding the best or only possible location in your home, you're ready for step 2.

Step 2: Supply Your Business Office

It's time to consider your office furniture and accessories. Make a scale model of possible configurations, using grid paper for the space and colored paper for the furniture and large pieces. Measure the room for your grid, remembering to indicate space taken up by windowsills and other protuberances. Mark windows, vents, phone jacks, switches, outlets, doors, and door clearances. When you choose business furniture and equipment, be sure that your doors, halls, and angles can accommodate them, and that there's room for them once they've cleared the access hurdles. You may need to buy smaller models, or double up with a fax/ copier or a phone/answering machine to save space. (See step 3 for some great space-saving ideas so your office can hold enough supplies to be self-sufficient.)

A self-sufficient office will make you more efficient. Going to another part of the house to borrow a stapler or answer the phone wastes your time and destroys your concentration. Check the list of furniture, accessories, and supplies earlier in this chapter for suggestions on what to stock. The nature of your business will determine which items you'll need more of, and what additional items you'll need.

Because you'll probably be using your business office more than you will your family office, educate yourself about ergonomics. The U.S. Occupational Safety and Health Administration (OSHA) takes the subject so seriously—especially given the high incidence (and cost) of carpal tunnel syndrome—that in 2000 it issued mandates for worker-friendly furniture, equipment, lighting, and other workplace features.

Lighting that's too dim, a desk that's too high, a chair that's made for another body type, or a keyboard or monitor that's awkwardly placed can seriously damage your eyes, back, neck, wrists, shoulders—even your overall health. Furthermore, your office—like the rest of your home—should be a healthy and pleasant place.

Design your work area to eliminate stress and discomfort. For example, if you refer to a document while you type, use a copy easel or clamp positioned so you can work without straining your eyes or your neck. Experiment with lamp placement and different types of bulbs to avoid eyestrain and headaches and to promote alertness. For all of these ergonomic concerns, consult the experts at furniture and lighting stores and try before you buy.

Step 3: Set Up Your Business Office

When setting up your office, refer to step 3 in the family-office section of this chapter. If you are light on space and heavy on "stuff," get rid of the stuff you don't need and purchase some space-savers to help you get and stay organized. To conserve floor space, go up! Install adjustable shelves from the floor to as far up as you can reach—higher if you have a step-stool handy. Adjust the distance between shelves so each shelf easily accommodates its contents without a lot of leftover vertical space. For the most efficient placement, store items of similar height together—but only if they belong together anyway. Look for sturdy paper organizers made to sit under computer printers; shelves designed to rest on monitors; grid racks to mount on walls, and wall pockets that mount on doors, cabinets, and—of course—walls.

Movable storage can be very helpful. Consider portable carts for hanging files. You can push the carts out of the way at the end of the day or week or when you have visitors. Another option, filing crates, are easy to take in the car and to store.

When setting up your files, refer to chapter 6, "The Paper Chase: Creating Files from Piles." You might want to add a tickler file, which "tickles" your memory so you don't have to think so much. Use it for items to be handled at a later time so you can concentrate on what has to be done right now. It's legal procrastination!

The tickler file, available in accordion-file or "book" form, is divided by days of the month or another time increment. It should be close to your workspace—in your drawer or on a shelf within reach—so you can refer to it regularly. Remember, you should note in your planner any item in your tickler file. For instance, if you need to take a form to a meeting on the 4th of the month, put it into the tab marked "4" and then note it on your planner on the 4th.

Subjects for business files might include clients, potential clients, product lines, advertising, marketing/promotion, office management, official business procedures, financial records, and other categories appropriate to your business. If you use a computer for business tasks, match the topics and subtopics of your computer files to those of your hard-copy files and arrange them accordingly. Color-code floppy disks and file folders.

For supplies, use carts with wheels, shelves, or drawers. You can find many storage items and ideas for your home-business office at office-supply stores, kitchen specialty shops, storage and container specialty stores, and discount department stores. Keep your eyes open whenever and wherever you shop! (And be sure to keep those receipts so you can deduct your business expenses!)

You can create an inexpensive, sturdy, and spacious workspace without nails, glue, duct tape, or rubber bands. I call it the "no-brainer" office desk. Buy two two-drawer file cabinets of equal height (about 29 inches) and a prebuilt Formica countertop available from large building-supply stores in 6-, 8-, 10-, and 12-foot lengths. (You'll need a third file cabinet for the longer lengths.) A little more than two feet deep, the counter will accommodate a computer and printer and lots of junk... organized junk, of course. The ideal thing about this setup is that you have "files at your fingertips."

When arranging storage, remember to keep the most-used items closest to your workspace. Ideally, you should not have to move or even to turn more than your arm or hand to retrieve them.

Keep your files, shelves, equipment, and supplies within reach. Consider one of three furniture arrangements:

▲ A U shape, with your desk in the lower part of the U.

▲ An L shape, with your workspace accommodating your right- or left-handedness.

▲ Two parallel rows you can conveniently access when sitting between them.

Whichever arrangement you choose, you'll be able to reach nearly anything you need by just turning your chair. A swivel chair helps with the turning part. If you miss the exercise involved in getting up and looking for things, consider taking up squash or square dancing. It's a better use of your time and more healthy!

As a rule, store like things together. Glue and tape and paste and clips are "stick-together things." There are also "things to write on," "things needed to mail something," and "things to write with." You can call the various categories anything you like; you don't have to use these technical terms.

Step 4: Set Up Your Business Communication Center

Your home business office needs a communication center, especially if you have employees. It's a designated place for the right hand to know what the left is doing...and when...and where...and vice versa. Adapt the ideas for your home communication center to your business. *Communication* is the key word here. Any reference books, notebooks, or product samples for common usage should be together in a designated place, accessible to all who use them.

Step 5: Set Up Your Business Desktop

It's important to be able to see the top of your desk. You don't need a photo of your kid or dog, nor do you need a dead plant in your office. Those can be in your living room. What you do need is uncluttered workspace. Apply the good habits of Leonard, Gladys, and Mary to your home business office when appropriate.

You might have only one computer for home and business use. Even so, separate personal items from business items, using separate disks, separate directories on your hard drive, and separate files. Store business and personal items separately;

use separate sides of the room, separate cabinets–ideally, separate rooms. There should be distinct lines akin to those you might have once created to keep your little sister out of your space. (You can learn a lot from your childhood.)

Now you're ready to go to work. The rest is all downhill!

Checklist: What You Learned

This chapter showed you how to do the following things:

❏ Find and clear a spot for your office
❏ Find or buy furniture, supplies, and equipment
❏ Arrange your furniture and equipment
❏ Put away office supplies
❏ Set up efficient working files
❏ Create a communication center
❏ Set up your desktop area
❏ Set up systems to handle household and family business
❏ Research home-business legal and insurance issues
❏ Set up systems for a professional office
❏ Determine which responsibilities to outsource

Now that you have organized your home and office, it's time to consider the children. Kids have a need to be organized so they can find their other tennis shoe or their math book. They also provide some organizing challenges for their care-takers! In chapter 8, we'll address both of these issues.

Chapter 8

Organizing *of* the Children, *by* the Children, and *with* the Children

Organizing is what you do before you do something, so that when you do it, it's not all mixed up.

–Christopher Robin in *Winnie the Pooh,* by A. A. Milne

Parents often ask me how to organize kids–meaning, they're ready for the school bus on time, fully dressed, backpack over their shoulders, and lunches in hand; able to master complex tasks such as putting their dishes in the sink after dinner; tidy enough to keep the health inspector at bay; and capable of doing their homework without three hours of negotiating. This scenario can't be realized with organization alone. It requires fostering mutual respect and teaching responsibility. Parents can "organize kids" only to a point. It's more beneficial to organize *with* your kids, encourage their creativity, entrust them with responsibilities, and allow them to experience the consequences (favorable or unfavorable).

Kids have their own ways of going about their business, as do adults. The way children handle responsibility is an extension of their personalities…as is true for adults. In varying degrees and in different situations, kids feel the need to be on time to soccer practice, to do well in school, to take care of their treasures, and to have their own space. Likewise, parents feel responsible for getting the kids to soccer practice, knowing what's going on in school, doing laundry, and preparing meals.

Teach Responsibility Every Day

Accountability is one of the most important things children learn, and they should begin learning it at an early age. They become responsible by being given the chance to fail.

As a parent, you can reinforce the lessons your children learn from failure. Ask your children (not gloatingly, but with concern) what happens when they forget their lunch money or can't find school papers. Ask how they feel when, due to *their* failure to take some responsibility, they can't be on a team because they were late for tryouts…or when they miss the bus for Worlds of Fun and can't go…or when the soccer team has to forfeit the game because they forgot to show up. Remind them that their actions, or inactions, have consequences…if not for them, for someone.

"Responsibility means learning from mistakes in an atmosphere of dignity and respect, not blame and shame," Jane Nelsen, Ed.D., explains in *Positive Discipline for Preschoolers*. "When we let kids experience the consequences of their choices and give them a chance to do better next time, then we're teaching them skills they'll need to handle future challenges. That's what responsibility is all about."[9] Kids do learn from their mistakes when parents don't bail them out. As one astute eight-year-old told me, "When things start being a problem, it's time to look at things different."

Decide how much responsibility you want your children to learn and at what ages; when should you stop reminding them to brush their teeth or take five egg cartons to school for a class project? Communicate the consequences of forgetting to feed the fish or tell you about an upcoming piano recital. Likewise, set a good example. Did you forget to tell them to eat lunch at school Thursday because you weren't going to be home? Admit your mistake, apologize, and discuss the consequences, just as you do when the error is theirs.

Communication: Talking and Listening

Good communication creates a sense of belonging and fosters skills for a lifetime: teamwork, problem-solving, cooperation, negotiation, and decision-making. You're all in this together, so discuss, as a family, ways to cope with chores, take care of belongings, arrange activities, and handle other responsibilities. Respectful communication helps kids become involved and feel important in the family unit. The more involved they are, the more important they become, and the sooner they understand the effect (positive or negative) of their actions on the family.

As kids and parents listen to each other and learn about each other's needs, they develop effective ways to juggle activities, share responsibility for the home and the meals, and find quiet time for reading or studying. You might find that some family members are overscheduled—that you need to review family priorities and reschedule accordingly.

Much of this chapter comes from the experts: a special group of 20 children between the ages of 6 and 16 that I call the OK Kids, for Organized Kind of Kids. Each OK Kid has his or her unique organizing styles. I actually began preparing for this research quite some time ago and as a result was able to contribute two of my grandchildren to the interview pool!

The OK Kids and I discussed their responsibilities in and outside the home, their spaces and places, their stuff, and their storage. Their ideas and techniques, along with those of other experts—moms, dads, professional organizers, and child psychologists—form the basis of this chapter.

Many of the OK Kids hadn't realized they had organizing systems until I asked about them—and in some cases, neither did their parents. They had developed creative ways to store their clothes and toys, take care of their rooms and pets, and do their chores and homework. Some had already learned that putting things where they belong means they don't have to spend time looking for them. An eight-year-old girl commented, "When I'm organized, I can find what I'm looking for pretty easy because I already know where it is before I start looking for it." A 10-year-old boy said, "If you don't have to spend time looking for something, you can get things done on time." And, speaking of time....

"I'm Late, I'm Late, for a Very Important Date!"

It's about time…as in time capsule, time machine, time crunch, time clock. It's time for dinner, it's time for school, it's time to brush your teeth. We pass time, kill time, take time, and waste time. Sleepytime, bedtime, central standard time….

At some point, kids begin to take responsibility for being on time to important activities. Either they learn now, or they become frustrated because they are always late to school, games, lessons, and other events. Maybe they don't tell their parents about their commitments until the last minute; or maybe parents drop the ball when they're responsible for transportation. Regardless of who's at fault, most kids really dislike being late. A 7-year-old told me that he likes to know a few days ahead of time when soccer games or other activities are coming up. A 12-year-old, who likes at least two days' notice for anything outside her routine, checks the family calendar next to the phone twice a day.

An expedient and almost painless way to avoid unwelcome surprises and communicate obligations is to establish a family communication center. Pick a spot that all family members pass on a regular basis—by the back door or the refrigerator or above the phone in the hall. This is the place for a *big* family calendar, where you can post dental appointments, scout meetings, and school vacations. It's fun and useful to assign each family member a different color. By color-coding activities, you can see at a glance whose schedule is especially busy; and kids are likely to pay attention to family calendar items written in their own special color. With a family calendar, kids can see when parents are unavailable and parents can arrange for transportation for the kids. It can be quite revealing to see the "busyness" of the family.

More items to post in the communication center (perhaps on a bulletin board next to the family calendar) include the following:

▲ Practice and game schedules

▲ Chores

▲ Phone and other messages

▲ Notes about what to take to school

▲ Forms to be filled out or signed

▲ Important and frequently called phone numbers

▲ Other vital information, such as what you want for your birthday or two-for-one dinner coupons from your favorite restaurant

You can leave messages for each other on color-coded sticky notes or on a dry-erase board. How about installing a wheel and attaching notes to it with clothes-pins–almost like the order wheels restaurants use? If the communication center is your refrigerator door, affix notes with magnets. Be creative, make it fun, and it will be more likely to be used.

Stock the communication center with little surprises or hidden treats; it might take a small bribe for the kids to remember to head toward it the minute they get home. Within a few weeks, it will become a habit.

Make it a morning habit, too. Checking the communication center early will get you and the kids on the right track for the rest of the day.

How Do You Start *Your* Day?

Relaxed or frazzled? Calm or crazy? Your morning mood is contagious. Often a bad beginning can mushroom into a lousy day for all. Starting off on the wrong foot–the disorganized one–leads to hasty decisions, hurried breakfasts, and a harried family.

The first step toward a peaceful, orderly morning is a familiar routine. Many of the OK Kids had established their own systems for starting the school day without undue stress. Here's what some of those 6- to 16-year-olds said:

▲ "I get up early to get every single thing done between 8:00 and 8:30 so I can watch my favorite show before I have to leave for school."

▲ "The night before, I take my schoolbooks and other stuff for school to a special place by the front door."

▲ "I set out my clothes the night before."

▲ "I take my shower at night instead of in the morning, when everyone competes for the bathroom and the hot water."

▲ "I get up two hours early to put on makeup, fix breakfast, curl my hair, and study."

More Ideas for Peaceful Mornings

▲ As a family, do a practice run of your morning routine, discuss ways to improve it, then do another run-through. Learn from each other. Keep practicing, discussing what works and why, until everyone is satisfied.

▲ Help your kids make a "picture chart" showing things to remember each morning or evening. They can draw pictures or cut them from magazines as reminders, adding check-off boxes if they want. In the morning or before bedtime, ask them if they've checked all their pictures (done their tasks).

What the Kids Can Do

If you get an evening routine going, soon it will become automatic. Once it becomes a habit, you'll have more time to play, read, daydream…and sleep.

Every night, do the following:

▲ Think about tomorrow; look at the family calendar and make sure you know what you have to do the next day, where you have to be, and how you'll get there.

▲ If you have homework, finish it, with papers ready to hand in.

▲ Put things you have to take somewhere—schoolwork, projects, your base-ball glove, piano music, lunch money, library books, your book bag—in a basket, bag, or box by the door.

▲ Get your clothes ready—all of them, including socks, shoes, and hair ribbons.

Moms and dads have to look at their calendars or planners, too—for the next day before they go to bed, and on Sunday for the week ahead.

Who Invented Chores, Anyway?

"If each one sweeps before his own door, the whole street is clean."

–Yiddish Proverb

Discuss the big picture—what it really means to belong to a family and "run the house-hold"—at a family meeting. Even if they don't like chores any better afterwards, the kids will understand why everyone has to do them.

Here are some of the points you might want to make:

▲ *You* don't always like doing chores either.

▲ When things aren't taken care of, they have to be fixed or replaced—leaving less money for family fun.

▲ A dirty house is a sick house. Regular dusting and vacuuming keeps down allergen levels—especially important for those with hay fever or asthma. Mold spores in kitchens, bathrooms, basements, carpets, and air ducts can make even healthy people sick.

▲ Pets that aren't brushed regularly can get flea-infested before you realize it. Ridding a house of fleas is expensive and time-consuming—and it's very hard work.

▲ In fact, the longer you put off any task, the harder it gets. It's much easier to rinse a dish right after eating than to scrape off dried egg or oatmeal or scrub a milk ring off a glass.

▲ If people slip on your icy sidewalk, they can be badly hurt (and even those with minor injuries have been known to sue the homeowner and win).

You don't need to lecture. Ask the kids to think of their own examples. What happens if toys aren't put away, pets aren't fed, plants aren't watered? What happens when they *are*? How are others (in and outside the family) affected? Why is it important for everyone to share the work?

When Are Kids Old Enough for Chores?

At what age should kids be given chores? As soon as they can follow directions. Toddlers can be guided to put some toys away before getting others out, and thus begin to form the habit of taking care of their things. Two-year-olds can put their dirty clothes in a basket or help stir the pudding. If you view these tasks as learning experiences instead of ways to lighten your workload, your kids might see their chores simply as part of the process of playing…and living. Let them experiment with their own methods (to a point).

As your children grow, you can

▲ Provide on-the-job training–and teach them the tricks of the trade.

▲ Ask for their suggestions–they might have a better way of doing something.

▲ Emphasize the importance of the task they're working on; explain how it fits into the big picture.

▲ Let them graduate from one task to another: from putting their dirty clothes in the hamper to prespotting to loading the washer to folding to ironing (yikes!).

Chore Tips for Parents

The parents I talked with had found a variety of effective approaches to chores and kids. Here are a few examples:

▲ Remind them that they're preparing for adulthood (they'll love that!). They'll probably say, "When I'm an adult, I won't make my kids do chores." Don't believe it!

▲ Break up chores into smaller tasks, such as sweeping one corner of the kitchen, then moving on to another corner.

▲ Jobs should fit the kids' ages and abilities; otherwise, they'll just get frustrated. One mother told me that her boys can dust if she takes all the stuff off the shelves. They can also gather the little wastebaskets from around the house and take their sheets off their beds to be washed.

▲ One family keeps chores and allowances separate. "They are totally different things," the mom explained. "One has to do with family responsibility, the other with money management."

▲ Privilege brings responsibility. "Mitch (age 2) doesn't have to help around the house, but he also can't go to the Family Fun Center," Mitch's dad told me.

▲ Work with children on new assignments until they understand what to do and how to do it.

▲ Encourage them to turn chores into a game.

What Do the Experts Do?

The OK Kids generally feel good about their skills and proud of what they do to help the family. (I wonder how often they tell mom and dad that!) I don't recall anyone being positively gleeful about chores, but several talked about them as a matter of course—as if to say, "This is just what we do in our family."

I asked the OK Kids for their chore lists. Here are some typical tasks they reported:

Six-year-olds hang up their PJs, make the bed, take out trash, pick out their own clothes, and get ready for school; "check the temperature so I know what to wear"; "put the rest of my lunch together while Mom makes my sandwich."

Seven-year-olds tend everything from the farm (feed hay to the cows, clean the barn, and rake) to the infirmary. They put dirty dishes in the sink, pick up their toys when they're done playing ("so my little sister doesn't get in my things"), and help set the table. Some entertain younger siblings "so Mom has extra time to do things; and when one of my parents is not feeling well, I make toast, cereal, and tea and take it in on a little folding table. I don't do that for my sister."

Eight-year-olds set the table, take dirty dishes to the sink and rinse them, help load and unload the dishwasher, vacuum, and tidy up their own and other rooms. ("If I don't put my things away when I play in some parts the house, Mom will throw them out.")

At **9, 10, and 11,** the OK Kids are doing the basics and more: "clean upstairs, bath, kitchen; dust," "rinse my own dishes after meals, sometimes sweep the floor, keep my things picked up around the house, shovel snow in the driveway." An 11-year-old told me that when she leaves things around the house for long, "Mom puts them in a big box and I have to do chores to get them back."

The **12- through 16-year-olds'** lists showed more diversity:

- ▲ "I have three rabbits, two birds, one fish, one frog. I do everything for them: feed, change cages, put tarps on cages when raining, give them flea baths."

- ▲ "I do my own laundry, change kitty litter, feed the cat, and do dishes all the time."

- ▲ "I fold laundry, clean floors, and sometimes clean the top floor."

- ▲ "I take care of my fish Calvin Klein. I feed him and clean the bowl."

▲ "I fish-sit for friends. They write out specific instructions (no, not the fish, my friends)."

▲ "I clean and wash windows, toilets, and my room; and I do my own laundry."

Parents: Help Yourselves

Here are some things you can do to make things easier around the house and reduce *your* chores:

▲ For health reasons, and so that you can tell whose towel is wadded up on the floor and growing mildew, assign each family member a separate set of towels (that are unlike the towels of other family members).

▲ Install towel hooks for everyone and put some low enough for the short guys. It's easier to hang a towel on a hook than to fold one over a bar, and just a little more difficult than dropping it on the floor.

▲ Put hampers or laundry baskets in each of the kids' bedrooms.

▲ Keep kids' dishes, and food they can get by themselves, in low kitchen cabinets.

▲ Hang kid-accessible soap and lotion dispensers in the kitchen and bathroom.

▲ Create a lunch station in your kitchen. Stock it with sandwich makings that don't need refrigeration, lunch-size packages of snacks, plastic bags, lunch sacks or boxes, napkins, and other necessities.

▲ Keep separate boxes or bins for each child's school papers you want to save. You might want to write the date on them.

Taking Care of My Space

OK Kids each have methods, ideas, and interests that are unique to them. Some are purposeful about how they take care of their things; some are more relaxed. Here are some of their ideas and observations, in their own words. I couldn't have said it better myself.

Age 6

▲ "I keep things in clear plastic boxes so I can see what's in the boxes. I also keep my Barbies and Polly Pockets in boxes so I can take them to friends' houses. Everything has a plastic box unless it's too big."

▲ "I can hang my own clothes up in the closet because there are lots of hooks and the rods are low. There's a place to hang my backpack on my door and for my shoes, my umbrella, and my jacket."

▲ "In my drawers I have underwear and socks, below that shirts (left side T-shirts; center, long-sleeved shirts; right side, sweatshirts). Then I have pants, then shorts."

Age 7

▲ "My room is not that organized but certain places in it are organized, like my desk…specific things in specific drawers: science drawer, reports and papers in file drawer, electronics in another. I have collections (rocks, pennies, buckles) in special cases so I can look at them, and I have junk. I put breakable things away. My treasures are my rocks with crystals; I built a little house outside for them."

▲ "I got to see a drawing of my new room–shelves, computer table, rug, bed, and dresser–and I helped decide where things would go in my new room. I wanted more shelves."

Age 8

▲ "I keep all my books together."

▲ "I keep my room picked up all along because I don't like to clean it up."

▲ "I know where most of my things are except if they're in my closet; things get lost in there."

Ages 9 to 11

▲ "I clean my room when I can't find something."

▲ "I hang sweaters, sweatshirts, and shirts and tank tops and vests in clusters."

▲ "I helped paint my room. I help take sheets off my bed and have special places for things so it's easier to not loose things."

Ages 12 to 16

▲ "When I clean my room, I pick up laundry first and put it in the hamper in my closet; then my shoes. I like to have fun and play 'cleaning talk show' to motivate me to clean my room. I try to make what I don't enjoy more enjoyable."

▲ "My closet is mostly organized. There are boxes with things and school clothes on one side of the closet, and with other clothes on the other side so when I need to get dressed I can grab it and go."

▲ "I put things in separate piles so it doesn't get confusing."

▲ "My room is kind of small and therefore more homey. I have posters and memorabilia on the wall. If my jeans are still clean, I put them away; I put dirty laundry in a basket in my room."

▲ "I made my own little filing cabinet for schoolwork, play scripts, and church stuff."

▲ "I can find my papers easily, but my hairbrush is usually buried under my clothes."

▲ "I like to organize to keep track of things. I organize my closet and drawers. Clothes I don't like to wear I put in the corner of the closet."

▲ "I have a special drawer in my room for school papers. I have special shelves in my closet and have my clothes divided up: socks, PJs, hair stuff, shorts, underwear. Long pants, short-sleeve shirts, and long-sleeve shirts are hanging up."

Space Capsules for Parents

▲ Remember to respect your kids' space. Their rooms are places to dream, create, and sometimes escape. Come to an agreement about how much mess you can tolerate, and why. (Is your child's room a health hazard? Are there visible fungi? Do you know where the gerbil is? Or is it harmlessly messy, inconveniencing only its occupant?)

▲ When planning a child's storage, get down on your hands and knees, or just on your knees, depending on the height of the child. Then try to reach objects and clothes; now try to put them away.

▲ Put clothes rods and hooks low enough for the kids to use. Hall trees, painted lockers, and low shelves are also handy for clothes storage.

▲ If too many toys accumulate on the floor of their rooms most of the time, put some away for later.

▲ When children are young, store puzzles and toys with small pieces out of reach until the kids want to play with them. Only one or two such toys should be out at one time so that pieces don't get mixed up. Have a basket for puzzle and game pieces that don't make it back into the box when you (or they) put the games and puzzles away.

Study Tips from the OK Kids

Help your kids find a way to organize their papers so they don't lose them or forget them, and provide a study area that is comfortable (but not too comfortable), well lit, and undisturbed. Efficient use of study time and good study skills will contribute to how well they learn. Naturally, getting their work to school, complete and on time, can only help their grades.

Given enough motivation—and a little latitude to innovate and experiment—kids will design their own systems for handling homework (and everything else). Many well-meaning parents insist that things be done "the right way" (read "my way"). Such an approach, if it works at all, cheats kids out of the joy of accomplishment and undermines the whole point of homework: to develop skills for, and a love of, learning.

It's certainly appropriate for parents to insist that homework be done and handed in on time, and to provide a setting, or choice of settings, in which their children can concentrate. It's at least as important to demonstrate, in word and deed, that while there are lists to memorize and tests to pass, the real reward comes when kids develop learning skills, intellectual curiosity, and interest in the world around them. Such children will never be bored. But those whose parents micro-manage the homework process or, worse yet, "help" too much when their kids get stuck, might never appreciate the priceless gift of education.

The Do-It-Yourself Method

When I was in elementary school, my father would not help me do my math problems; he told me he didn't learn that in school. Then he proceeded to ask me a series of questions until I came up with the answers. I not only learned the math, I understood the process. My father, by the way, was a CPA...and a very wise dad.

Homework Hints from Junior-High Students

Our junior-high experts have come up with their own clever and effective ways of handling homework. Here are some of their unique approaches:

▲ "I use the Swiss Cheese approach; I study little bits at a time until the homework is all gone...or done. If you don't like to study for long periods of time, study a little after breakfast and a little after lunch."

▲ "I can study 20 minutes on one subject; then I lose concentration and have to move on to another."

▲ "I do math first when I'm most alert, because it's the hardest for me."

▲ "I read the whole assignment, then I reread it, especially the hard parts; sometimes I take notes."

▲ "I do homework assignments on Friday afternoon and evening so I can go to church youth group on Sunday night."

▲ "When I don't want to study, I go into Marcy's room and say 'tell me to study' and she says, 'Hanna, study,' and I go in my room and do it."

More OK Kids Advice

▲ Be aware of assignments and what's on the test. Ask your teachers questions.

▲ Get a mentor or friend to study with you.

▲ While studying, listen to soft music, to the radio, some classical music—or work in complete quiet—whatever helps.

▲ Have your mom, dad, sister, brother, or friends quiz you before a test.

▲ Sit where you'll be comfortable for as long as your homework takes—at a desk, on your bed, or in a light, bright place on the floor. Or choose different places to sit for different subjects.

There's No "Right Way"

Sometimes very dissimilar processes give equally good results. With a school homework project, for example, one of the OK Kids sizes it up at the beginning and waits until later to begin. Another one starts it the day it's assigned and sets due dates along the way for different parts of the project.

They organize their papers and their assignments differently. One uses an assignment notebook to record long-term, daily, and extra-credit assignments. One keeps completed assignments in a designated folder, separate from her other school papers; she keeps this folder in her backpack. Another keeps papers in a Trapper Keeper with a different folder for each subject. Yet another keeps completed and returned papers in a portable filing crate until the end of the school year. She throws most of them away after she receives her final grades. She has a file drawer for special projects and exceptionally interesting assignments she wants to follow up on.

Beyond encouraging your kids to create their own customized study space, and making sure they have good light and essentials such as pens, paper, and reference books, you as a parent have a limited role in your children's homework. With the kids, remembering that you're the parent, decide on appropriate limits concerning phone use when there's homework to be done; also remind them to put their backpacks by the door when finished. Express interest in what they're learning; offer to arrange a family field trip to the observatory if they're studying astronomy.

There is one more way you can help: Show them how to organize with color-coding. Teach them as toddlers to keep their coloring books in a red box and their drawings in a yellow box. Not many years down the road, they'll be putting their algebra papers in a blue folder and their English papers in a red one, and they'll always be able to locate them quickly.

Summary of Important Kid-Organization Points

Remember, organizing with kids is a matter of listening to and respecting them, creating learning opportunities, and sharing your own needs and those of others in the family. Set aside time to communicate regularly and frequently. Be patient and persistent when they balk, and soon your kids will be more than organized–they'll be well on the way to becoming responsible, competent, and self-assured young adults.

The last chapter will give you an opportunity to list your own important records. Complete and maintain these records in a way that would be helpful in the event of your illness or disability.

Chapter 9

For the Record

This chapter is for recording vital personal information for quick reference. Review this information annually and keep it in a safe place. (Refer to chapter 6 for suggestions on storage for related documents and relevant papers.) Your family members should know about the record and its location. Remember, "A less-than-perfect record-keeping system is better than no system at all."[11]

How This Chapter Is Organized

This chapter is divided into four sections:

▲ Section 1: Personal and Family Records

▲ Section 2: Personal Property

▲ Section 3: Financial Information

▲ Section 4: Final Wishes

Section 1: Personal and Family Records

Use this section to record information about yourself and your family members. You may need these records when filling out school cards, camp forms, scholarship applications, resumes, and other documents. There is an eight-page form on which you can record information about your name, birth date and place, health, marriage, education, employment, organizations, honors, awards, and military service. You should fill out a form for each member of your family.

Items Covered in This Section

- ▲ Name
- ▲ Birth date and place
- ▲ Parents and siblings
- ▲ Social Security number
- ▲ Religion
- ▲ Marriage
- ▲ Passport

- ▲ Health
- ▲ Education and training
- ▲ Honors, awards, interests
- ▲ Military service
- ▲ Employment and skills
- ▲ References
- ▲ Organizations you belong to

Section 2: Personal Property

This section is for recording saleable valuables such as antiques, jewelry, art, collections, furs, or coins. You may also include automobiles and real estate you own and use other than as investments. There are two lists for you to keep up-dated: items in your safe-deposit box and items in your wallet, such as credit cards, driver's license, or bank cards. The latter is helpful in case you lose your wallet.

Items Covered in This Section

- ▲ Real estate
- ▲ Automobiles
- ▲ Other personal property: jewelry, antiques, collections, furs, coins, artwork

- ▲ Safe-deposit box contents
- ▲ Billfold contents

Section 3: Financial Information

This section is where you record information on your investments, insurance policies, retirement plans, savings, loans, checking accounts, debts, and what is owed to you.

Items Covered in This Section

▲ Investments

▲ Retirement plans

▲ Savings accounts

▲ Insurance

▲ Financial institutions: accounts

▲ Credit cards

▲ Debts

▲ Money and objects on loan

Section 4: Final Wishes

This section is for recording procedures and instructions you want followed when you die, as well as whom to notify and the location of wills, trusts, and other vital information.

Items Covered in This Section

▲ Whom to notify immediately

▲ Disposal of body (burial, cremation, donation to science)

▲ Planning the service: funeral, memorial service, wake, graveside service, military or lodge service

▲ Special bequests

▲ What to do within a few weeks of the death

Section 1: Personal and Family Records

Personal Information

Legal Name:	First	Middle	Last		Maiden	Nickname

Birth:	Birth certificate number			Date (DOB)	month	day	year

Adoption Information:

Place of Birth:	County	Town or city		State	Country

Facility or Address:

Doctor:

Parents:	Mother	Father

Siblings:

Social Security Number: __ __ __ - __ __ - __ __ __ __	Religion:

Marriage:	Date	Place

Full legal name of spouse

Passport:	Number	Expiration date

Health Records

Blood type	**Eyeglass prescription**	
Allergies	**Severe illnesses**	
Disabilities	**Special medications**	

Inoculations/Vaccinations:		
Type	Date	Doctor/clinic

Surgeries:		
Type	Date	Doctor/clinic

Education from A to Z

School/Location	Dates Att.	Yr. Grad	Major	Degree
Grade school				
Jr. high or middle school				
High school				
Higher education				

Other Training

Workshops

Seminars

Educational honors and awards

Special interests

Military Service:
Name, dates of service, branch, rank, serial number, insurance & death benefits, honors, medals, discharge dates, location of papers.

Employment and References

Place of Employment

Address/city/state

Phone	Dates	Supervisor or manager

Type of work done	Skills acquired & extra training

Place of Employment

Address/city/state

Phone	Dates	Supervisor or manager

Type of work done	Skills acquired & extra training

Place of Employment

Address/city/state

Phone	Dates	Supervisor or manager

Type of work done	Skills acquired & extra training

Place of Employment

Address/city/state

Phone	Dates	Supervisor or manager

Type of work done	Skills acquired & extra training

Place of Employment

Address/city/state

Phone	Dates	Supervisor or manager

Type of work done	Skills acquired & extra training

Place of Employment

Address/city/state

Phone	Dates	Supervisor or manager

Type of work done	Skills acquired & extra training

References

Name	Title	
Business/organization		Phone
Address/city/state/ZIP	Other pertinent info	

Name	Title	
Business/organization		Phone
Address/city/state/ZIP	Other pertinent info	

Name	Title	
Business/organization		Phone
Address/city/state/ZIP	Other pertinent info	

Name	Title	
Business/organization		Phone
Address/city/state/ZIP	Other pertinent info	

Organizations I Belong to

Name of organization

Type of organization

Membership number/date of joining

Other information

Name of organization

Type of organization

Membership number/date of joining

Other information

Name of organization

Type of organization

Membership number/date of joining

Other information

Section 2: Personal Property

Real Estate			
Location			
Size of property	**Value**	**Date of evaluation**	**Date of acquisition**
Mortgage(s)		**Description**	
Location			
Size of property	**Value**	**Date of evaluation**	**Date of acquisition**
Mortgage(s)		**Description**	
Location			
Size of property	**Value**	**Date of evaluation**	**Date of acquisition**
Mortgage(s)		**Description**	

Automobiles and Other Vehicles

Title		

Registration #		

Make	Model	Color

Year	VIN #	

License plate: state & number		

Title		

Registration #		

Make	Model	Color

Year	VIN #	

License plate: state & number		

Title		

Registration #		

Make	Model	Color

Year	VIN #	

License plate: state & number		

Title		

Registration #		

Make	Model	Color

Year	VIN #	

License plate: state & number		

Other Personal Property

Jewelry, antiques, collections, furs, coins, art
(Record any pertinent information, including value, when assessed, and by whom.)

_____

_____

_____

_____

_____

_____

_____

_____

_____

_____

_____

_____

_____

_____

_____

_____

_____

_____

_____

_____

_____

_____

_____

Safe-Deposit Box(es)

Location of	Authorized person(s)
Number	Location of keys

Contents
(Include dates, registration numbers, serial numbers, or other official-looking data and any other identification.)

Papers you should keep in your safe-deposit box or strongbox:
List of insurance policy numbers, companies, and amounts of insurance; copy of will; list of government bonds and serial numbers; proof of repayment of debts; deeds to property; mortgage papers; leases; marriage certificates; birth certificates; military discharge papers; corporation stock certificates and bonds; car titles; passports; other legal or valuable papers.

_____

_____

_____

_____

_____

_____

_____

_____

_____

_____

_____

_____

_____

_____

Billfold Contents

Driver's license: State, county			Number	

Bank cards, credit cards, insurance cards
(Under "Phone #," put the number to call in case the card is lost; you can find this information on your statement.)

Type of Card	Issued by	Account Number	Exp. Date	Phone #

Other important contents to report in case of loss or theft:

Section 3: Financial Information

Investments
List locations of stocks, bonds, real estate transfers, or other investments.

Brokerage house or company

Address

Contact person	Phone

Description

Brokerage house or company

Address

Contact person	Phone

Description

Brokerage house or company

Address

Contact person	Phone

Description

Retirement Plans

Type of plan	Company to contact

Address

Contact person	Phone

Description

Type of plan	Company to contact

Address

Contact person	Phone

Description

Type of plan	Company to contact

Address

Contact person	Phone

Description

Savings Accounts

Name and location of account

| Account number | Phone |
| Type of account | Interest rate |

Other

Name and location of account

| Account number | Phone |
| Type of account | Interest rate |

Other

Name and location of account

| Account number | Phone |
| Type of account | Interest rate |

Other

Your Homeowner's or Renter's Insurance

In case of fire or robbery, make lists and take pictures of the contents of your home or apartment, or make a videotape with voice descriptions. Include date of purchase, cost, make, model, and serial numbers when appropriate. You can update your records annually with photographs, receipts, and written descriptions. When you take photos or videotapes, open closet doors, put appliances on counters or tables, and include all valuables.

Have the following valuables appraised: jewelry, collections, antiques, furs, computers, artwork, and gold and silver pieces. Whenever possible, etch your Social Security number on the backs of appliances, electronic equipment, computer equipment, and other machinery. In case of theft, notify your law enforcement agency of your number and give the agency a list of these items.

Insurance

(Automobile, Health, Homeowner's, Renter's, Liability, Life, Personal Property)

Type of coverage	
Policy number	Amount
Insurance company	Address/phone
Insurance agent	Address/phone
Policy issued to:	

Type of coverage	
Policy number	Amount
Insurance company	Address/phone
Insurance agent	Address/phone
Policy issued to:	

Type of coverage	
Policy number	Amount
Insurance company	Address/phone
Insurance agent	Address/phone
Policy issued to:	

Financial Institutions: Accounts

Type of account (checking, savings)
Account number + PIN
Name of institution
Address/phone
Type of account (checking, savings)
Account number + PIN
Name of institution
Address/phone
Type of account (checking, savings)
Account number + PIN
Name of institution
Address/phone

Type of account (checking, savings)

Account number + PIN

Name of institution

Address/phone

Type of account (checking, savings)

Account number + PIN

Name of institution

Address/phone

Type of account (checking, savings)

Account number + PIN

Name of institution

Address/phone

Credit Cards			
Name/Address of Business	Identification Number	Name of Cardholder	# to Call in Case of Loss

Debts

Name/Address of Lender	Type of Debt	Identification Number	Due Date

Money and Objects on Loan

Name/Address of Borrower	Object or Amount Due	Due Date	Interest	Location of Document

Section 4: Final Wishes

Keep this book, completed, in a fireproof, safe place, but not in a safe-deposit box because it couldn't be accessed immediately following a death. Make sure a few trustworthy people know about this book and its whereabouts.

Procedure and Instructions

In the event of my death, please read this section thoroughly before notifying anyone.

1. Notify the Following:		
	Name	**Address**	**Phone**
Doctor or coroner			
Clergy or officiating authority			
Funeral director and cemetery			
Relatives			

(continues)

(continued)

	Name	Address	Phone
Relatives *(continued)*			
Close Friends			

	Name	Address	Phone
Place of employment			
Attorney			
Accountant			
Executor of estate			
Others			
Newspaper (may be done by clergy or mortuary)			

2. Disposal of Body (Burial, Cremation, Donation to Science)

I wish to be	
I have made plans with	
I have a burial plot at	

(continues)

(continued)

3. Planning the Service (Funeral, Memorial Service, Wake, Graveside Service, Military or Lodge Service)

The type of service I want	
Location	
Music	
Clothing and objects (in case of burial)	
Other requests	
Family information needed immediately	
Father's full name	
His birth date	**His birthplace**
Mother's maiden name	
Her birth date	**Her birthplace**
My full name	
My birth date	**My birthplace**
My Social Security number	
Other information for obituary	
Location of will	**Date of will**

Special Bequests

Item and Family Significance	To Whom

Within a Few Weeks of the Death

You will need a copy of the death certificate for items 1 to 8.

1. Open safe-deposit box and examine contents.

2. Have bank, savings, and loan accounts released.

3. Contact insurance companies.

4. File will (see attorney about this).

5. Transfer titles to stocks, bonds, mutual funds, and other such documents.

6. Transfer real estate titles.

7. Arrange for pension payments to be made.

8. Contact Social Security office about payments and death benefits.

9. Contact accountant and/or attorney about inheritance taxes, income taxes, and other financial and legal matters.

10. Contact department of motor vehicles about vehicle ownership.

11. Contact credit card issuers and issuers of other accounts.

12. Cancel any periodical or other subscriptions.

13. Contact clubs, lodges, and other organizations.

Checklist: What You Learned

This chapter showed you how to do the following things:

- ❏ Gather important data for personal business
- ❏ Create or update records
- ❏ Devise a system for periodic updating

You have now completed your record-keeping, as well as your organizing. Write to Pipi Peterson, c/o JIST Publishing. We will send you an application for a Certificate of Accomplishment for all of your hard work and good organization!

Notes

1. R. Alec MacKenzie, *The Time Trap,* Third Edition (New York: AMACOM 1997).

2. Charles B. Inlander and Cynthia K. Moran, *Stress: 63 Ways to Relieve Tension and Stay Healthy* (New York: Walker and Company, 1996).

3. David B. Sudderth, M.D., and Joseph Kandel, M.D., *Adult ADD: The Complete Handbook* (Rocklin, CA: Prima Publishing, 1997).

4. Judith Kolberg, *What Every Professional Organizer Needs to Know About Chronic Disorganization* (Judith Kolberg and FileHeads Professional Organizers, 1999).

5. Judith Kolberg, *Conquering Chronic Disorganization* (Decatur, Georgia: Squall Press, Inc., 1999).

6. Edwin C. Bliss, *Getting Things Done: The ABCs of Time Management* (New York: Bantam, 1993).

7. Stephen R. Covey, *The Seven Habits of Highly Effective People: Powerful Lessons in Personal Change* (New York: Simon & Schuster, 1990).

8. Don Gabor, *Big Things Happen When You Do the Little Things Right* (Rocklin, CA: Prima Publishing, 1997).

9. Jane Nelsen, *Positive Discipline for Preschoolers* (Rocklin, CA: Prima Publishing, 1998).

10. Donna Goldfein, *Everywoman's Guide to Time Management* (Millbrae, CA: Les Femmes Publishing, 1977).

11. Barbara Hemphill, *Taming the Office Tiger* (Washington D.C.: Kiplinger Washington Editors, Inc., 1996).

Glossary of Terms Used in This Book

Here are the special terms and definitions that will help you in your quest for organization. The chapter number at the end of some entries denotes the chapter in which the word or concept is described most fully. When the term is a worksheet used in the book, we also provide the page number where you can find this worksheet.

activity. An individual step toward a goal or objective. (Chapter 1.)

Annual Agenda. A record of responsibilities and events that recur once or a few times a year, or less often (for example, servicing the heating-cooling system twice a year, or painting the house every five years). (Chapter 2, page 42.)

business office. See *home business office*. (Chapter 7.)

calendar. This book discusses several types of calendars, including the family calendar and the annual calendar. (Chapters 3 and 7.)

Clothing Worksheet. A categorized list of your family's clothing and proposed storage. (Chapter 5, page 95.)

communication center. A conveniently located place in your home where your family leaves and picks up messages and notes, consults the family calendar, views schedules for the season's soccer games or symphony concerts, and so forth. (Chapters 7 and 8.)

deep storage. Placement for documents (and other items) that must be kept but that are rarely referred to; includes safe-deposit boxes and out-of-the-way storage areas in your home; also called *level-one storage*. (Chapter 6.)

desktop storage. Placement of items that you continually refer to (also called *level-four storage*). (Chapter 6.)

family calendar. A prominently displayed (in the communication center) record of upcoming activities and commitments, ideally color-coded according to family member. (Chapters 7 and 8.)

family communication center. See *communication center.*

family office. In this book, the headquarters for conducting household and family business, as distinguished from your home business office, which is where you conduct a business enterprise. (Chapter 7.)

filing crates. Portable file-storage boxes resembling plastic milk crates but fitted with grooves for suspending hanging file folders. (Chapter 6.)

Financial Matters. Documents, notes, and other papers dealing with household financial concerns; one of three major document categories (the others being *Memorabilia* and *Household and Family Business*). (Chapter 6.)

goal. Destination; desired achievement; the purpose of and framework for activities. (See also *objective.*) Ideally, goals are closely aligned with priorities and principles. (Chapter 1.)

home business office. The place in your home where you conduct a business enterprise, as distinguished from your family office, which you use for household and family matters. (Chapter 7.)

Household and Family Business. Documents, notes, and other papers dealing with your home and family; one of three major document categories (the others being *Memorabilia* and *Financial Matters*). (Chapter 6.)

household inventory. A record of valuable, irreplaceable, or difficult-to-replace possessions; to be used for insurance documentation and as a reference for family members. (Chapter 4.)

Item Category List. A worksheet summarizing your family's possessions, their classifications, and their current and proposed storage. (Chapter 4, page 78.)

level-four storage. See *desktop storage.*

level-one storage. See *deep storage.*

level-three storage. See *ready reference.*

level-two storage. See *occasional reference.*

Memorabilia. Keepsakes–documents, notes, and other papers (and sometimes other types of items) dealing with concluded events, activities, and so forth; one of three major document categories (the others being *Financial Matters* and *Household and Family Business*). (Chapter 6.)

Monthly Agenda. A record of responsibilities and events that recur every other month or once or twice a month (for example, paying bills on the 1st and the 16th, or cleaning the clothes-dryer vent every 60 days). (Chapter 2, page 46.)

objective. An intermediate goal. The words *goal* and *objective* can be interchangeable, but in this book *goal* refers to a desired achievement and *objective* describes a subordinate achievement in pursuit of a goal. For example, if your goal is to reach Walla Walla by Tuesday, a related objective might be to arrive in Boise tomorrow night. (Chapter 1.)

occasional reference. Storage for documents used once or twice a year; more accessible than deep storage but less so than ready reference; also called *level-two storage*. (Chapter 6.)

OK Kids. Organized Kind of Kids; the 6- to 16-year-olds who served as consultants for chapter 8; also, all young people who purposefully and creatively arrange their time and belongings and participate in family responsibilities. (Chapter 8.)

planner. Planning calendar; your principal reference for appointments, errands, and other plans and commitments. It can be anything from a desk calendar, to a wall calendar, to a fancy leather-bound planning system. (Chapter 3.)

principles. Values, ideals, morals; the beliefs you live by. (Chapter 1.)

priorities. Elements of your life that are most important to you. *Priorities* and *principles* are closely related. For example, among your priorities might be family, public service, and an organized household, proceeding (respectively) from principles such as loyalty, duty, and harmony. (Chapter 1.)

ready reference. Storage for documents used frequently but not daily; more accessible than occasional reference; also called *level-three storage*. (Chapter 6.)

Storage List. Summary of available storage areas and items in your home. (Chapter 4, page 82.)

to-do list. A synopsis of phone calls to make, projects to work on, errands to run, and upcoming activities and appointments. (Chapter 3.)

Weekly Agenda. A record of responsibilities and events that recur once or twice a week. (Chapter 2.)

Index